France and the Second World War

Occupation, collaboration and resistance

Peter Davies
University of Huddersfield

London and New York

First published 2001
by Routledge
11 New Fetter Lane, London EC4P 4EE

Simultaneously published in the USA and Canada
by Routledge
29 West 35th Street, New York, NY 10001

Routledge is an imprint of the Taylor & Francis Group

Typeset in Sabon and Gill Sans by
The Running Head Limited, Cambridge
Printed and bound in Great Britain by
TJ International Ltd, Padstow, Cornwall

British Library Cataloguing in Publication Data
A catalogue record for this book is available from the British Library.

Library of Congress Cataloging in Publication Data
Davies, Peter Jonathan, 1966–
    France and the Second World War: occupation, collaboration and
resistance/Peter Davies.
        p.   cm. – (Introduction to history).
        Includes bibliographical references and index.
        1. France – History – German occupation, 1940–1945.   2. World War,
    1939–1945 – Underground movements – France.   3. France – History –
    1945–   I. Title.   II. Series.
    D802.F8 D32   2000
    944.081'6—dc21   00–036591

ISBN 0–415–23897–8 (pbk)
ISBN 0–415–23896–X (hbk)

This book is dedicated to my beautiful baby niece, Emily

Contents

Preface

I would like to thank the following people: Heather McCallum, Luciana O'Flaherty and Gillian Oliver at Routledge for their enthusiasm and support, and Bill Roberts and Derek Lynch at the University of Huddersfield for their extremely helpful comments on specific chapters.

I also wish to offer my sincere thanks to the University of Huddersfield – for its financial help; and to all the historians I have quoted and referred to – for their provocative and fascinating insights into the subject of occupied France.

And, finally, I would like to acknowledge the commitment and enthusiasm of all the undergraduate students at the University of Huddersfield who have taken my module on wartime France and who have enthused me so much.

Peter Davies
Huddersfield, February 2000

Chronology of key events

1939

March	Czechoslovakia is occupied by Germany.
April	Lebrun is re-elected as President.
21 August	The Nazi–Soviet Pact is formed.
25 August	Communist publications are banned by the French government.
1 September	Poland is invaded by Germany.
3 September	Britain and France declare war on Germany.
26 September	The French Communist Party is dissolved by Daladier.

1940

29 February	The introduction of ration cards.
20 March	Daladier is succeeded by Reynaud as premier.
28 March	The Anglo-French agreement, prohibiting either country from making a separate peace with Germany, is formed.
10 May	The Low Countries are invaded by Germany.
13 May	The German forces enter France by crossing the Meuse.
18 May	Reynaud becomes Minister of National Defence; Pétain enters government.
5 June	De Gaulle becomes Under-Secretary of State in the Ministry of War.
14 June	The German forces enter Paris. The French government moves to Bordeaux.
15 June	The fall of Strasbourg and Verdun.
16 June	Pétain succeeds Reynaud.

17 June	Pétain calls for an armistice; de Gaulle flies to Britain.
18 June	De Gaulle makes a radio broadcast from London calling for resistance.
22 June	The Franco-German Armistice.
23 June	Hitler travels to Paris; Laval becomes Pétain's Deputy Prime Minister.
28 June	Britain recognises de Gaulle as leader of the Free French.
30 June	The Vichy regime creates the *Chantiers de Jeunesse*.
1 July	The French government moves to Vichy.
3 July	The British attack the French fleet at Mers-el-Kébir.
5 July	The Vichy regime breaks off diplomatic relations with Britain.
10 July	Pétain is voted full powers; the end of the Third Republic.
11 July	Pétain becomes head of state.
3 August	Abetz is appointed German ambassador in Paris.
September	The Free France expedition to Dakar fails.
27 September	Germany demands a census of Jews in the occupied zone.
3 October	The Vichy regime passes the first law on Jews.
24 October	Pétain and Hitler agree on collaboration at Montoire.
13 December	The end of the Laval ministry.

1941

February	Darlan takes charge of the government.
22 June	Germany invades the Soviet Union; the beginning of French communists' resistance effort.

1942

February	The creation of the *Milice*.
15 February	The Vichy regime declares abortion to be a crime against the state.

March	The first groups of Jews are deported from France to concentration camps.
April	Laval returns to government.
8 November	The Allied forces land in Morocco and Algeria.
11 November	The Germans move into the unoccupied zone.
24 December	The assassination of Darlan.

1943

January	The *Mouvements Unis de la Résistance* (MUR) is formed.
Winter	Maquis groupings start to form.
February	The *Service du travail obligatoire* (STO) is introduced.
May	The *Conseil National de la Résistance* (CNR) is formed.
June	The *Comité Français de Libération Nationale* (CFLN) is formed in Algiers under stewardship of de Gaulle and Giraud.

1944

January	Paris-based collaborationists join the government.
6 June	The Allies land in Normandy.
15 August	The Allies land in southern France.
20 August	Pétain is moved to Belfort.
25 August	The Liberation of Paris.
26 August	De Gaulle arrives in Paris.

1945

7 May	The Germans surrender.
July	The trial of Pétain.
21 October	The end of the Third Republic.

1946

| January | The resignation of de Gaulle.[1] |

Introduction

Background and context

This book seeks to introduce the reader to an important and highly controversial period of French history: world war and occupation. It is a short but intriguing era: one that is constantly being revisited by historians and one that has an enduring appeal for students. It is a period that keeps throwing up important debates and one that refuses to go away (its legacy has been particularly evident throughout the 1980s and 1990s – as we will discover in Chapter 5). It also incorporates a fascinating array of themes: fascism, war, collaboration, resistance, and civil war.

It may be helpful here to sketch out the main contours of the period under consideration. France entered the Second World War in 1939 but within months she had suffered a catastrophic military reverse at the hands of Germany. In June 1940 the Franco-German Armistice was signed; and after the defeat-induced collapse of the Third Republic, Marshal Philippe Pétain assumed power. With Germany occupying the north of France – including Paris – the 'independent' French government moved first to Bordeaux and then to Vichy.

For the first two years or so, the Vichy administration had some autonomy, but after 1942 and the German invasion of the southern zone all this changed and the occupiers were, effectively, in control of the whole country. While they had some leeway to govern, Pétain and a succession of right-hand men – most famously, Laval – initiated a range of policies. The showcase development was the National Revolution. In the three spheres of '*travail, famille, patrie*', the Vichy administration attempted to return France – or the southern zone at least – to its traditionalist past. And, in a voluntary manner, it also agreed to co-operate with the German occupiers in a range of areas. Most

1

horrifically, the Pétain-led administration played its part in the Holocaust. Although there is much debate as to the exact role of France and the French in this initiative, it is clear that Pétain, Laval and others were, for the most part, willing accomplices in the project.

At the same time, a myriad of groups – both inside and outside France – were forming and evolving with the explicit aim of resisting the German presence in France and opposing the Vichy regime. Outside France resistance took the form of de Gaulle's Free French movement; inside, it had a million and one different incarnations: from the highly organised Communist Party, through an array of smaller political organisations, to the anarchic and terroristic Maquis movement and to individuals up and down the country who expressed their dissatisfaction, hurt and anger at the German occupation in many and various ways. (As we will discover, it is extremely hard to generalise: there were as many different types of resistance as there were resisters; the same could also be said of collaboration.)

Ultimately, these forces, in tandem with the Allied powers, were able to help extricate France from the despair and shame of the Occupation. And in 1944, through the Liberation – so full of hope, but also so full of problems – France emerged, at last, from the trauma of world war and the Occupation. But in what state did she emerge? Other questions will also challenge us over the forthcoming pages. For example: What factors explain the Fall of France? Why was France occupied? Which political ideas and values did the Vichy regime embody? Why did France collaborate? And, moving on to other important aspects of the wartime period: Who resisted, and why? What were the main social and economic consequences of the war? Who liberated France? How should we think about, and interpret, the legacy of the Occupation period? These questions and debates will preoccupy us – just as they have preoccupied a host of post-war writers.

It is no surprise that the Occupation period has provoked historians and commentators so pointedly. In the early days – during the war and just following it – the literature on the period was, not unnaturally, highly politicised. On the whole it was devoid of real hindsight and balance. In the two or three decades after the Liberation, and as the Gaullist 'resistance myth' came into conflict with the less charitable myth of France as 'a nation of collaborators', there was little of a challenging nature written about the Occupation period. There was Aron's history of Vichy[1] and a whole range of de Gaulle-centred histories, starting with his memoirs and moving on to a variety of biographical studies; but for most of the time, with the myth of France as 'a nation of resisters' still prominent, and with post-war France generally unable, or unwilling, to face up to the unpleasant reality of the era, it could be argued that the political climate was not exactly conducive to genuine historical enquiry.

This, however, began to change in the 1970s. *The Sorrow and the Pity* – a documentary film which challenged, in an explicit fashion, the validity of the Gaullist myth – appeared at the start of the decade,[2] as did Paxton's ground-breaking study of Pétain's regime, *Vichy France: Old Guard and New Order 1940–1944*. In his introduction to this book, Paxton talks about the way in which the 1970s heralded a 'new curiosity'[3] about the Vichy regime and witnessed a significant opening-up of official archives. With the ascension of the socialist Mitterrand to the presidency in 1981 *and* with the further passing of time, the climate seemed to change for the better. A void appeared to open up; and into it, with relish, appeared historians like Hoffman (Vichy), Kedward (the Resistance), Halls (Vichy youth movements), Kuisel (the economy), Marrus and Paxton (the Jews), Collins Weitz (women), Burrin (the Occupation) and Rousso (Vichy and memory). A new wave of war trials (Barbie, Bousquet, Touvier and Papon) and a fresh outpouring of literature and cinematic work also seemed to be symptomatic of the new climate. And, as one might suspect, this new surge in artistic work and historical enquiry did not please everyone.

To comprehend the wartime period, however, one must first appreciate the climactic nature of the Fall of France – described variously as a 'debâcle', a 'disaster' and a 'catastrophe'.[4] In essence, the fall of France is an umbrella term that covers both military and political demise.[5] It centres on a series of key events in 1940:

10 May	Germany invades the Low Countries.
13–14 May	The French front is broken on the Meuse.
18 May	Reynaud becomes Minister of National Defence in place of Daladier.
19 May	Gamelin is replaced by Weygand; Pétain enters government.
29 May–4 June	The evacuation from Dunkirk.
10 June	The French government moves to Touraine; Italy enters the war.

14 June	The Germans enter Paris; the French government moves to Bordeaux.
16 June	The resignation of Reynaud and succession of Pétain.
18 June	General de Gaulle calls from London for continued resistance.
22 June	The Armistice with Germany.
24 June	The Armistice with Italy.
1 July	The French government moves to Vichy.
3 July	The British attack on the French fleet at Mers-el-Kébir.
10 July	The National Assembly votes full powers to Pétain.[6]

It is extremely difficult to analyse the Fall of France in 1940 without making reference to the political and economic tribulations of the previous decades, and so an understanding of the inter-war years is crucial to an overall analysis of 1940. Of course, at the root of it, the Fall of France was a disastrous military episode, but it is also wrapped in social, economic, political and perhaps even psychological significance.

The Great Depression and the Crash of 1929, together with fascist riots in 1934 and the emergence of the Popular Front in 1936, helped to create a weak and divided France – a France torn by left–right tension and prone to extremism on both flanks of the political spectrum. As a consequence, it could be argued that France's foreign policy and international standing was affected adversely and thus, that in 1940, she was not ready to stand up to Germany.

This, of course, was most obvious on the military plane. Cobban states that the defeat of France in 1940 was a military defeat pure and simple and that the collapse of the nation was synonymous with this.[7] The argument here is straightforward: bad organisation, out-of-date military tactics and a general unpreparedness led, extremely rapidly, to defeat.[8] Mixed in with this, many historians allege, was a tremendously blasé attitude: a belief that, somehow, trench warfare could triumph over *blitzkrieg*, and also that defence spending did not have to respond to political developments in Germany. On this last point, it is interesting to note that expenditure on defence actually *fell* in the 12 months following Hitler's accession to the chancellorship. And even though it rose in 1935, the damage seemed to have been done; and perhaps more importantly, the French establishment had revealed its rather backward and unenlightened attitude.

It is easy to detect a definite arrogance in the stance taken by the French authorities. Many people seemed to take the view that because France emerged a victor in 1918 she would do so again – without much effort – in the second major world conflict of the century. In this sense, it is argued by some that, for France, a victory was much harder to overcome than a defeat. The nation and its people had claimed a massive triumph after Versailles – but at the same time they had failed to realise that it was the USA's contribution to the First World War that had been decisive and that France herself had been desperately weakened by the conflict. In crude terms, France – post-1918 – was living in a fantasy world: she was far weaker than she actually thought she was. Horne argues that the Maginot line – and more significantly, the 'Maginot line mentality' – was a particularly unfortunate symptom of France's inter-war attitude.[9] This is where the psychological dimension to the country's malaise clearly becomes apparent: a dimension that should not be underestimated.

It could also be argued, quite strongly, that France's foreign policy[10] in the period 1919–39 was weak and incoherent. Part of the problem was that her diplomatic stance was constantly changing: from strong anti-Germanism in the immediate post-war period to the desire for 'mutual guarantees' in the late 1920s; and from the early-1930s, quest for security in the face of Hitler to appeasement in the latter half of the decade. Foreign policy-making was schizophrenic – there was no real consistency and no convincing central thrust. As Cobban points out, France was impotent in the face of Nazi adventurism and increasingly over-dependent on Great Britain in particular in the diplomatic sphere. He also claims that in the inter-war period the nation was divided on everything except the need to avoid a second world conflict – sadly ironic given the course of history after 1939.[11] There was certainly a strong defeatist feel to French foreign policy in the pre-war years; diplomatic impotence was a definite symptom of demise and decline, and ultimately foreshadowed military defeat and political collapse.

The sense of domestic crisis in 1930s' France was also a key contributory factor. The right's interpretation of the Fall of France rests almost exclusively on the belief that 1940 was the 'fault' of the Third Republic and the politicians who, in their eyes, came to personify it.

At the time, this argument was advanced by Pétain. His main claim was that the disaster of 1940 was merely the reflection of the Third Republic's political defects on a military plane. Many aspects of the post-1871 regime were condemned: the 'excessive' power of parliament over government, the adverse effects of proportional representation, and the continual instability brought on by regular elections and changes in government. Away from the polemic and rhetoric implicit in the right's critique, there was some substance to the attack. For instance, between 1914 and 1940 there were numerous changes in prime minister. As a result, it was alleged, France lacked the opportunity to develop long-term policy perspectives in a whole range of spheres.

It is also undeniable that inter-war France was beset by terrible political feuding and in-fighting. It was a divided society, but also a polarised one. On the left, there was a real awakening: in 1924 the *Cartel des gauches* gained power and 12 years later the *Front populaire* entered government. On the right, there was a profound radicalisation: the growth of the fascist *ligues* – and the events of 6 February 1934 – signifying a serious new threat to the Republic. Pétain's claim was that France was divided and unstable, and thus could not possibly prevent, or cope with, a situation like 1940. For him, politicians and the infrastructure of the Third Republic were to blame; his 'solution' was firm, executive and almost monarchical government.

Another view is that national economic decline prepared the way for military defeat, even if it did not directly cause it. The view here is that economic stagnation in the inter-war period created a situation in which France was unwilling, and perhaps unable, to make a stand against Germany; military defeat and political collapse followed on. There were disturbing signs: imports had outgrown exports, tourism was declining, the franc was falling, and the country's dependence on reparations was increasing (in a period when Germany was endeavouring to pay less and less). There was also population stagnation – an extremely serious development in a country that had always established a definite link between reproduction levels and national prowess. All these trends were serious in themselves but together, in economic and psychological terms, they had a devastating effect on France's national health.

This book will explore, and synthesise, the main secondary writings on the Occupation period; in certain places too, the spotlight will shift to key primary sources. The structure of the book will be thematic, although where appropriate the period's chronology will be highlighted. In Chapter 1, the Occupation – the backdrop to collaboration and resistance – will be examined as a social, economic and political phenomenon. As such, this section will explore the everyday reality of the Occupation and the main economic and societal trends at play.

In the following two chapters the 'high' politics of the period will be explored. In Chapter 2, the Vichy regime and the policy of collaboration will be assessed. These two topics are, arguably, the most contentious aspects of the Occupation era. In Chapter 3, the phenomenon of resistance will come under the spotlight. What were the different types of resistance? Who were the resisters? What was the ideology of resistance? Throughout, we will be very conscious of the fact that there was never, really, one such thing called 'the Resistance'.

In Chapter 4, the focus will shift to the Liberation. Here there is one dominant, and crucial, debate: who liberated France? This historical controversy will be looked at in detail. A picture of the Liberation era will be painted via the many important themes at play in the elongated period that was the Liberation. The last section – Chapter 5 – will take a different slant on the wartime period: its legacy. The ramifications of the period for post-war France should not be underestimated. It has left an indelible stain on the psyche of modern France – a stain that is still extremely evident.

CHAPTER ONE

Occupation

French and Germans

A feeling of rape (*Un sentiment de viol*)
Henri Frenay on the Occupation[1]

The Occupation of France was heralded by Article 1 of the Franco-German Armistice, signed in June 1940.[2] This notorious document announced that Germany would be occupying northern and western regions of the country; approximately 35 million French people would, therefore, have to live under direct German tutelage. Agulhon talks about the occupied zone as the 'third quarter of the disjointed nation'.[3] Kedward argues that, initially, French people thought of the Occupation in military terms only and 'did not envisage it in either political or economic terms',[4] while Larkin says that the attitude of most French people was 'stunned acceptance'.[5] In the second half of 1940, the Nazis launched a systematic campaign of pro-German, anti-British propaganda.[6]

By 1942 Germany had moved into the southern zone. The Occupation was, by then, complete. We must remember that occupation was not a new experience for France. She had suffered the same fate, albeit for much shorter durations, in 1814, 1871 and 1914. Occupation 1940-style, however, was to be on an altogether different scale. In time it was to become a military, social, economic, political and psychological reality; and it would leave an indelible stain on the nation's psyche.[7] Naturally, the Occupation had an immediate and varied impact. The most obvious effect was dislocation. As German troops swarmed into France, a mass of people 'emigrated' from the north to the south. This 'exodus' involved women and children primarily and, in the decades since, has gained mythical status; in photographs and newsreel film it has been depicted graphically.[8] Ousby has explored this theme further and called his chapter on the Occupation: 'Presence and absence'. Alluding to the writings of Sartre, he declares:

> The occupation began by demanding that people accept the fact of presence, the presence of a foreign conqueror in their midst. Yet increasingly it demanded that they also reconcile themselves to the fact of absence, or rather to a series of absences which began with the disappearance of friends, neighbours or fellow-citizens and pointed towards a vacancy of the spirit, an engulfing nothingness.[9]

At its most stark, the Occupation meant a climate of fear and suspicion. Larkin claims that there was a safe 'middle ground' between resistance and collaboration but that, in practice, everyone was in a state of 'moral disarray'.[10]

However, it would be a mistake to view the Occupation, solely, as a crude Nazi strategy – as, if you like, 'France under the swastika'.[11] Of course, in many ways this was what the Occupation was all about; but, in another way, the Occupation can be viewed as a clever and subtle strategy. For, splitting France in two was a brilliant example of 'divide and rule' thinking in action. Creating an 'independent' southern zone was a definite tactic. In essence, from the German standpoint, the thinking was: give the French some independence, let them squabble among themselves, and let us not exert unnecessary energy on governing areas of France that have no great economic utility. Kedward expands on this point:

> The division between the zones which had seemed a thin line on a map was gradually seen for what it really was, a military frontier which the Germans could close or open at will, and in the first weeks after the armistice it was opened only to selected workers and administrators whom the Germans decided were vital to the smooth recovery of basic industries and public services in Paris and the north. By leaving as many people as possible to French initiatives in the south, the Germans ensured that grievances about food and other provisions were directed against French rather than German authorities. It was part of their tactics for maximising the effects of the war and defeat for which the French

would be held responsible, and minimizing the effects of the Occupation which could be held against themselves.[12]

The Germans ruled France via a military governor. He had large freedom of action in both political and economic domains. In general though, he had only one aim: to maintain order and stability. He was aided by staff in Paris and the regions, and also by a well oiled police and propaganda machine. These were important dimensions to the German presence in France, but the key relationship was that between the Military Governor and the German Ambassador in Paris, Otto Abetz. What existed, therefore, was a kind of cabinet-style operation: the Military Governor and the Ambassador working in tandem with a small group of councillors. Together, they possessed a good working knowledge of France and French affairs.[13]

In the next chapter we will examine the Vichy regime and the policy of collaboration, and in Chapter 3 we will explore the reality of the Resistance, in all its diversity and plurality. In these two chapters, the 'headline' political issues will be examined and important insights will be gained into the nature of both political 'factions' and, through this, into the nature of the profound fault-line that existed in wartime France. This chapter, however, will focus on the political, military, social and economic undercurrents of the Occupation. There are three main issues: *Origins:* why did the Occupation take place? *Reality:* what did the Occupation mean in practice? *Implications:* how should we assess the effects, consequences, and legacy, of the Occupation?

So, in this chapter the nature and everyday reality of the Occupation and the social and economic effects of the German invasion will be considered. For the most part, the situation in the occupied zone will interest us. Occasionally though, it will be helpful to take a more holistic view of the Occupation; at times, therefore, it will be useful to take examples and illustrations from the southern unoccupied zone.

Beginnings

How and why did Nazi Germany commence its Occupation? More specifically, what was the rationale behind the policy? What was Hitler's tactical thinking? What was the significance of the Armistice and the ramifications of the Montoire meeting?

The Armistice of June 1940 was an event tinged with vengeance. Hitler held the meeting with Pétain in an old railway carriage – an explicit reminder of the 1918 meeting when the roles were reversed and France was in the ascendant. At the start of the chapter we looked at the military ramifications of the Armistice. Here we will examine the aspects of the Armistice which shed light on the Germans' 'philosophy' of occupation, and also those features that can broaden and deepen our understanding of what occupied France, in reality, was like. To sum up: what can the Armistice tell us about the nature of the Occupation?

It is clear, first, that the Occupation was a strategic measure. Article 2 of the Armistice makes this plain: it is not that France is being occupied for the sake of it, or for purposes of revenge, but rather, 'to assure the protection of the interests of the German Reich'.[14] In this sense the Occupation was a tactic, one part of Hitler's European master plan. The Armistice goes on to state, and define, the role of the occupier:

> In those regions of France occupied by the Germans, the Reich is to exercise all the rights of an occupying power. The French Government undertakes to assist in all ways the carrying-out of orders made for the execution of these rights and to have them put into force with the help of the French administration. Consequently, the French Government is immediately to notify the authorities and public services of the occupied territories that they will have to conform to the decisions of the German military commanders and to collaborate faithfully with them. The German Government will give to the French Government and to the central administrations all facilities for putting into force the administration from Paris of occupied and unoccupied territory.[15]

This, as one can see, is an extremely clear statement of intent. As Simon intimates, 'France' was a worthless, hollow term after the Armistice.[16]

The Armistice was not particularly specific about what the day-to-day reality of the Occupation would be. Perhaps only a quarter or so of the Armistice terms dealt directly with social and economic matters; the rest of the articles were avowedly military in substance. Nevertheless, the raft of non-military terms do go some way to substantiating the view that sees the Armistice as a particularly harsh, vindictive document. The key word is subservience. The French might have been hoping for some kind of partnership; but what they got, in the end, was a servant–master relationship.

This is most vividly illustrated in Article 18: 'The cost of maintaining German troops in French territory falls on the French Government.'[17] This was blanket liability – France was to pick up the tab for the whole Occupation. Other significant duties were put the way of France (or what was left of it). It had to 'assure across unoccupied territory the transit of goods between the German Empire and Italy to the extent required by the German Government' and also to 'undertake the repatriation of the population in the occupied regions'.[18]

There were thus obligations – and also restrictions. Article 17, for example, states that there must be no transport of 'securities and foodstuffs' from occupied territory into unoccupied areas; and further, that the French government[19] will guarantee this. Likewise Article 14 stipulates that: 'With regard to the French broadcasting stations, a restriction on transmitting will immediately be put into force.'[20] Not everything, though, was put down in black and white. The Germans, after all, had licence to do as they pleased, to make up the rules of the Occupation as they went along, and to dictate terms, continually, during the wartime period.[21]

Reality

The reality of the post-Armistice situation was symbolised by the 'line of demarcation'[22] which separated occupied France in the north from unoccupied France in the south.[23] It eventually disappeared, but this should be viewed as an indicator of *total* occupation rather than as any kind of German 'concession'.[24] While it existed, the line remained a visible reminder of national division. Sweets comments:

> The major crossing-point closest to Clermont-Ferrand was located at Moulins, north of Vichy. Before its suppression on 1 March 1943 . . . this boundary was a major irritant to the French. Because their country was divided by closely watched internal frontiers, they were forced to communicate with friends, relatives, or business associates on regulation postcards and letters subject to German interception and censorship. During the first year of the Occupation, travel between the two zones was restricted

severely by German authorities, and occasionally traffic was cut off entirely to pressure the French in negotiations concerning the application of the Armistice terms.[25]

So 'the line' was a real-life symbol. And Paris – the capital of the occupied zone – was akin to a 'vast German garrison town'.[26]

There are other important questions: What did the Occupation mean in practical terms? How did France, and ordinary French people, respond to the Nazi invasion? What was the nature of French-French, French-German and German-French relations during the wartime period?

Kedward paints an extremely vivid picture of the Occupation's initial impact:

> Those returning in July to their homes in the occupied zone found all tricolour flags removed from public buildings and replaced by Nazi insignia, street directions in bold German type, a curfew imposed from eight o'clock in the evening to six in the morning, total absence of French cars and lorries, and groups of Germans everywhere buying lavishly in the re-opening shops, riding from one tourist site to another, staging endless parades and holding concerts in the local bandstands . . . Shopkeepers had to accept the German currency and were obliged to serve Germans first, though not all German soldiers insisted on this.[27]

In the crudest of terms, the Occupation can be characterised as an exercise in control and exploitation.[28] In this sense, there was massive, and acute, disruption; in another sense, French people just got on with their day-to-day lives and were unaffected. This is the paradox inherent in the Occupation: there was both change and continuity and, in the words of Nettelbeck, 'disillusionment and illusions . . . abjection and hope'.[29]

Most obviously, the Occupation had severe economic effects. Defrasne has described the Occupation as an 'economic pillage'[30] and in reality it would be difficult for anyone to disagree with this verdict. The bare bones are these: France's index of industrial production fell from 100 in 1938 to 54 in 1941 and 33 in 1944; meanwhile the index for agricultural output fell away from 100 in 1938 to 69 in 1944.[31]

France was exploited mercilessly for the good of the German war effort. The occupiers altered the whole *raison d'être* of the French economy for selfish reasons. Production, distribution and exchange were all affected. Cobban talks about the 'Nazi exploitation of France':

> This took many forms. Occupation costs were raised after the invasion of North Africa, from 300 to 500 million francs a day. The vast amount of credit which the German authorities accumulated in this way was used for the acquisition of raw materials and food stuffs, French securities and works of art, for payments to the dependants of French workers recruited for labour in Germany, and to finance all the civil and military services of the occupying power . . . The Germans insisted on a policy of controlled wages and prices. This resulted in the growth of a vast and nation-wide black market, which the occupying authorities themselves tolerated and used with an appropriate rake-off . . . Behind the financial exploitation of France, which was largely a matter of book-keeping, there was the reality of systematically stripping France of raw materials, food stuffs, and manufactured products.[32]

As regards the everyday reality of the Occupation, there are a score of fascinating indicators. The figures below relate to Paris only:

Milk consumption (litres)
1938   7m
1942   3.6m

Bread prices (francs per kg)
1938   2.70
1942   3.70
1945   7.40

Meat in circulation
1938   68,000 tons
1945   24,000 tons

Increase in cases of TB
1939–41   30 per cent

Cost of living
Up 166 per cent in 4 years

Power of franc (by index)
1939   1.07
1942   0.60
1945   0.295[33]

These statistics lead to one main conclusion: life in occupied France was expensive and often unhealthy.[34]

Food was a particularly crucial issue. In a time of war, and of Occupation, this was always going to be the case. Collins Weitz states:

> For most, food was *the* primary concern in France throughout the occupation. One can appreciate the impact of major food shortages in a country where meals are the focus of daily life. Bread and meat were rationed by the end of September 1940; other commodities were added to the list of rationed products shortly thereafter. Allocations – determined by age and activity – diminished during the occupation years. Simone de Beauvoir was among the many women for whom concerns about finding food became a major obsession during the war years: 'I watched while the coupons were clipped from my rations books, and never parted with one too many. I wandered through the street rummaging ... for unrationed food stuffs, a sort of treasure hunt, and I thoroughly enjoyed it.'[35]

Sweets cites the example of Clermont-Ferrand. He quotes two local police officers: one speaking before the Germans moved into the south, another afterwards:

> The situation of numerous households, workers or lower civil servants has become truly precarious in the face of the unbroken rise in the cost of living ... The situation would be disastrous had there not been created happily at Clermont-Ferrand numerous workers' gardens which are helping to overcome many difficulties ... For many products the black market has become the only market ... Potatoes are impossible to find. One never sees them in the regular markets because of the regulated prices that have

been set . . . really much too low. What is abundant is sold at very high prices, what is rare is still higher.[36]

The working class . . . and in a general manner . . . those retired on modest incomes . . . are suffering more and more . . . The basic necessities are being sold at higher and higher prices and will soon be entirely beyond their means.[37]

Even in the south, the consequences of the Occupation were clear.[38] More generally, the pressure of dislocation affected the very nature of the French economy.[39] There was barter, rationing and the emergence of an extensive black market.[40] Agulhon states:

The Germans were now physically present everywhere. Economic impositions aggravated the hardships. Everything was rationed, everything was in short supply, there were food ration cards, monthly allocations of 'coupons', 'points' to authorize the purchase of small quantities of goods of all kinds; official provisions, which were often mediocre, were sometimes lacking because the available stocks had vanished from the legal circuits to resurface on the black market.[41]

One artist even sketched a drawing of women queuing for lipstick.[42]

On another level there was the *service du travail obligatoire* (STO): a scheme which obliged France to send nationals to Germany to work for the Nazi regime. Initially France sent 250,000 men and women, including around 150,000 specialists; by 1944 the overall figure had risen to about 1,000,000.[43] Cobban says that 'by the autumn of 1943 it was estimated that French workers constituted one fourth of all foreign male workers in Germany'. In essence the STO was an economic diktat with which France had to comply. It had severe consequences; most obviously, the imbalance between German and French economies was enhanced. In social terms, it created a situation in which families and couples were broken up – often for good. It also forced people to make up their minds politically. As Agulhon states: 'It imposed on several thousands of young people the clear choice between active collaboration by leaving for the STO, and active resistance, by refusing. It offered the maquis an unexpected and substantial recruitment pool.'[44]

In social terms, the Occupation had a wide array of ramifications.

From the appearance of dark, bold German type on signposts and buildings to the reality of 11 p.m. curfews, the impact of the occupiers was ever-present. There were scores of German-French male–female liaisons – a 'crime' for which many native women were to pay come the Liberation – and also, interestingly, a marked increase in the number of French people partial to wearing red, white and blue clothes. This 'act' was viewed as one of the most basic forms of resistance, and also as one of the most effective in terms of boosting French morale – in just the same way as the 'act' of giving inaccurate or misleading directions to German soldiers was. Far more sinister though were the notices which started to appear saying: 'OUT OF BOUNDS TO JEWS'. Suddenly, French people had to make it their business to sign special declaration forms indicating that they were *not* Jews or freemasons.[45]

The dislocation implicit in war and the Occupation also had a range of significant demographic effects. Once again, these statistics relate to Paris only:

Births
1938   32,645
1940   23,511
1941   26,513

Deaths
1937   33,571
1941   37,095

Marriages (French to French)
1938   27,000
1944   13,000

Suicides
1940–44   down by 50 per cent

Alcoholism
1937–40   average of 33,000 alcoholics in institutions
1943–45   average of 20,000 alcoholics in institutions[46]

These figures require some explanation. It is clear that the experience of war discouraged people from getting married. Similarly, the figures

17

for births and deaths are completely understandable given the decrease in marriages and the loss of life that accompanies war. Most intriguing perhaps are the figures for suicides. Here it is argued that the experience of war – and the ultimate hope of liberation – stopped many people from taking their own life. According to this line of argument, war gave people something to live for; so, bizarrely, misery *before* the war encouraged more suicides than it did *during* the war. One positive effect to come out of the war was the decline in alcoholism. Rationing had at least one advantageous outcome.[47]

In the sphere of communications the German presence was extremely evident. In addition to symbolic developments – all French clocks were set to German time, thus flummoxing and unnerving a good proportion of the indigenous population – the occupiers started to control and censor 'French' publications. *Le Matin*, for example, was one of the first newspapers to sell out (metaphorically rather than literally). Gradually, however, pro-German, pro-Nazi propaganda began to seep through the whole of the Paris-based media. Transport was also affected. The Germans requisitioned 4,000 out of a total of 17,000 locomotives and 294,000 wagons.[48] Metro stations were closed for large chunks of the wartime period and post and rail services were also seriously cut. The occupying forces constantly stated that the railways would resume normal operations, but in 1944 it was a fact that more than half of all rail traffic was German-orientated. And for various economic reasons, many people used bicycles instead of cars. As Ousby states:

> Though traffic had not vanished from the streets of Paris, the change was eerie to anyone who remembered the city before the war. An observer who conducted his own amateur survey toward the end of 1943 counted, during a ten-minute period near midday on the Place de la Bourse, just three cars, a motorbike and a horse-drawn cab.[49]

The Occupation affected the normal daily routines of ordinary people; freedom of circulation was limited and an *Ausweis* – a special German pass or 'internal passport' – was needed for even the most basic of journeys within the northern zone (or between zones). This general lack of movement had interesting, and diverse, consequences: the number of car accidents decreased – less movement meant less cars and, thus, less accidents – and the life of rural inhabitants became increasingly isolated.

Likewise the German presence had not insignificant consequences for leisure.[50] The occupiers tried to create an artificial life for themselves – at the races, theatre and so on – and this added to the strange and surreal atmosphere. Cinemas closed in the afternoon; they generally showed a subtle cocktail of French films and German news propaganda. Many onlookers also noted the fact that French nightclubs were packed with Germans – a feature of life that de Beauvoir, in particular, highlights.[51]

The Occupation was also a period of massive, and profound, artistic creation.[52] One view is that the period 1943–44 was the richestever for art – especially in Paris.[53] The forces of the Resistance placed an especially high premium on the *political* power of art. However, many intellectuals allowed themselves to be compromised, and continued working in 'Germanized' Paris.[54] Artists such as Van Dongen, Vlaminck, Friez, Despiaux, Bouchard, Derain, Le Jeune and Belmondo have all been branded as 'collaborators'.[55]

In addition, the Germans made significant efforts to promote themselves and their country. As Burrin writes:

> The so-called 'educated' public was . . . being targeted in other ways. It was presented with a prodigious collection of the most sophisticated products of German culture: a curious idea, it might be thought, at a time when the two countries were still in a state of war and the clash of arms was to be heard on all sides.[56]

Burrin suggests that the occupiers were particularly successful in promoting their music, their language, and – via a series of lectures at the German Institute – aspects of their history and way of life.[57]

Politically, the occupied zone was a strange mix. The Germans and their representatives obviously held sway, but resistance groups were emerging throughout the wartime period. There was also an extra, unpredictable element: the Paris Nazis. These people – cranks and misfits for the most part – were based in the capital and although their real political significance was minimal, they were an interesting group: zealous admirers of the Nazi regime, and at the same time harsh critics of the Pétain administration. That said, the Germans looked upon them as lightweights. It is also true that some individuals moved *between* the Paris salons and the Vichy government. Politically, and geographically, therefore, the Paris-based fascists were caught between the two political centres. Agulhon states:

> The occupied zone had its own political situation, by all the evidence more sensitive to the war and therefore less vulnerable to the illusions of that free and almost normal France which Vichy would 'doctor' with its own 'remedial treatment'. Above all, Paris was a pole of influence over which Vichy had hardly any hold.[58]

Underlying everything, however, was the experience of ordinary men and women. In the context of occupied France, however, there is no such thing as 'women's experience' any more than there is 'men's experience',[59] but even so it is clear that women, more than ever, became 'involved' in politics and in the making of political choices. They also suffered. Collins Weitz quotes Evelyne Sullerot on 1940:

> My mother was not with us when the Germans suddenly invaded France. She had gone to see my twenty-year-old brother who had been mobilised. Do you have any idea of what that means? . . . They came at night. We heard strange noises and voices. It was the Germans installing guns in our garden. So it was that one night I heard that language which I came to hate to such an extent that it is impossible to express. My grandmother (who knew German) told us, 'Those are the Germans.' It was extraordinary. They entered our garden; just like that. They seemed to belong to another race. It was a Panzer division. The soldiers were very tall – almost six feet – and dressed entirely in black with skull-and-crossbones insignias.[60]

It could be argued, therefore, that women bore the brunt of the dislocation heralded by the Occupation and war. And, on the evidence of Sullerot's words, their view of the German occupiers was typical of the French population as a whole.

We started this section by making reference to the 'line of demarcation' which split the northern zone from the southern zone and which inevitably came to symbolise national division. The Occupation has also attracted other depictions. Ousby emphasises the theme of darkness:

Darkness, which would prove one of the most common practical inconveniences of the occupation, was also from the first its symbol. The late daybreak on winter mornings and the power cuts which robbed homes of light: these were not just irritations or hardships that soon grew commonplace. They were identified with the occupation on a quite elemental level. Darkness, or so people at first feared, was like the darkness which visited the people of Egypt in the Old Testament: a sign of divine disfavour, that the gods who had once smiled on the nation had now indefinitely withdrawn their protection.[61]

We should also be aware of other ways in which the Occupation has been characterised. In many poster images during and after the war, the Occupation was likened to slavery, submission and subservience. As such, France – German-controlled France – was portrayed as a vulnerable and enslaved woman.[62] On the same kind of theme, the notion that France was 'raped' and 'violated' by the Occupation has gained currency.[63] 'Silence' too has emerged as a pertinent metaphor for the Occupation.[64]

The German presence

Underlying all of this was the presence of the Germans. At its most brutal, the German presence meant significant police activity via the Gestapo.[65] The Gestapo in France was made up of approximately 2,000 men and officials. For most of the time, and particularly in the hours of darkness, the Gestapo was feared; the presence of its officers made everyone anxious, and instantaneous arrests often accompanied its operations.

The presence of the Gestapo had its effect. In addition to arrests, the organisation was notorious for its hostage-taking (although this gradually declined) and its 24-hour-a-day torture chambers. The military tribunals manned and operated by the Gestapo were the most explicit indication of its philosophy. These 'courts' were ready to rubber-stamp summary executions for even the most mundane of 'anti-German' acts. For most of the time the French police worked together with the German police.[66]

The Gestapo attempted to regulate the life of the occupied zone. It

21

closed down the university in Paris as a retort to anti-German protests and, on an altogether more routine level, announced that French people had to cross roads at appointed places. Its activity in occupied France was influenced and conditioned by a variety of factors: the demands of Berlin, the political climate in Paris, the outlook of the military governor and ambassador, and also the course of the war outside France.

Throughout the Occupation period, the Franco-German dynamic was fascinating to observe. Here were two mighty nations engaging in a new type of relationship: partners in collaboration, with the victors on the battlefield dictating terms to the vanquished. Quite naturally, this new arrangement had all kinds of ramifications. On the whole, Germany viewed France as a weak and impotent nation, and the country's military and diplomatic staff tended to view a posting to the occupied zone as a passport to an easy life, particularly when compared to the challenges, and dangers, of life on the eastern front.

For its part, France had a somewhat schizophrenic view of Germany and Germans. On the one hand, it was very easy for French people to depict Germany as a nation of Nazis. This attitude was common and understandable, hence the broad-ranging efforts at resistance – from the most organised to the most petty-minded and innocuous. Not unnaturally, there was also particular venom reserved for the Germans' anti-Jewish policy. On the other hand though, and perhaps quite surprisingly, many French people came to realise that the 'Nazi occupiers' were ordinary, normal people after all. This comes out in many different spheres. In *The Silence of the Sea*, the main message seems to be that, however much the uncle and the niece want – and are expected – to hate their German lodger, they actually quite like him: he's decent, cultured and friendly. At the end of the film, when the niece does eventually speak to the officer – she utters one word, '*Adieu*' – it is symbolic of an extremely significant coming-together (perhaps even of a romantic nature).[67] Similarly, in the writings of de Beauvoir, it is possible to see a grudging, and perhaps growing, respect for the Germans she encounters in her everyday life.[68]

Of course, de Beauvoir hated the whole notion of the Occupation – calling it at one point, 'absolutely hellish'[69] – but she begins to admire the Germans' kindness, politeness and general decency. For her, the fact that the Germans *were* so cheerful, while at the same time the French appeared so miserable, made the whole experience of the Occupation so much worse. Sweets puts forward another perspective. He says that what existed was a kind of apartheid, with German officials and representatives of the French government receiving special treatment in all kinds of ways.[70] That for him was the reality of the Occupation.

More than anything, the Germans' presence had consequences for the northern zone's Jewish population. As Agulhon states: 'It was in Paris that the Jews caught the full force, and with the least chance of flight or protection, of the lash of Nazi anti-Semitism, marching towards the "final solution".'[71] Thus, from May 1942 onwards Jews in Paris were obliged to wear a yellow star to denote their identity. Round-ups followed.[72] The irony was that early on in the war many Jews were totally unaware of the horrific fate that would eventually subsume them. Adler states: 'It was physical survival that was at stake for the Jews of Paris during the Occupation yet few Jews realised this soon enough.'[73] In the end it was the Berlin decree of 1942 – ordering mass deportations – which forced them to open their eyes.[74]

The Occupation was, therefore, a terrible ordeal.[75] Ousby might argue that the Occupation was 'unnatural' and that 'the Germans never belonged',[76] but the bottom line was simple. As Collins Weitz puts it: 'Those in the occupied zone, where collaborationists were in charge, *had* to deal with the German presence.'[77]

Division

The main legacy of the Occupation was division. One can examine this on a variety of levels. Division had a very definite geographical basis. Not only did the perennial Paris/Provinces quarrel re-open, but the urban–rural split also returned to France. Sartre says in his writings that during the war, Parisians – by nature of the fact that they were living so close to 'the enemy' – were habitually accused of collaborating; southerners meanwhile were attacked by northerners for leading an easy, blasé, life (by 1942 though, when the Germans invaded the southern zone, this tension was, for obvious reasons, no longer evident).[78]

The traditional urban–rural friction – always on display, even at the best of times – had a similar kind of tone: the urban areas felt that the countryside was starving the cities.[79] As Collins Weitz comments:

City dwellers 'rediscovered' their country cousins. Reports from different regions reveal a growing contrast between rich and poor, between city dweller and peasant. Peasants were viewed as privileged, although this was hardly true for those with small holdings. City dwellers tended to believe the peasants received good prices for their crops and sold on the black market as well. While some did profit from the country's predicament, other peasants generously helped the Resistance with food and shelter.[80]

Sweets also confirms that towns and cities in the southern zone, like Clermont-Ferrand, 'bore less of the *direct* costs of defeat and Occupation than was the case for those French cities more exposed to large-scale military engagements and four years of total Occupation'.[81] This should not come as too much of a surprise. Ousby concludes that:

> On the whole people fared better in rural areas than in great cities like Paris. In the countryside, people were better placed to produce for themselves, exchange with their neighbours, forage for food or fuel and, of course, to conceal produce from requisitioning.[82]

The Occupation did nothing to bring different classes closer together. On the contrary, it created profound tensions. The working classes knew that they had suffered most during the 1939–40 conflict; they also knew that they had borne the brunt of the STO. As a result, they argued that some groups – most notably, the upper classes – had hardly been affected at all. As Ousby states:

> By the terrible logic of the occupation, the French who went hungry kept most of their anger for the French who ate well . . . The have-nots, which meant most of the French, did not have to visit expensive restaurants to find . . . filthy rich to despise, such *arrivistes* to resent. They could find them in profiteering shopkeepers who, like the Poissonards, charged ridiculous prices or tried to fob them off with unsaleable goods.[83]

There was a similar split between generations. On the whole, the veterans of the First World War blamed the young for losing the war in 1940; the young retorted by saying that the writing had been on the wall since 1918 when the older generation had 'lost' the Versailles peace. It was mentioned earlier that, in an important sense, the Germans thrived on the division that, on a national scale, the Occupation brought. And, inadvertently, they also benefited from the many socio-economic divisions that the invasion and the reality of the Occupation crystallised.[84]

In summing up, it is helpful to refer to a cartoon of a café scene in a wartime French newspaper. The image featured two people: a waiter and a customer. The dialogue was as follows:

> Customer: 'The usual please, garçon.'
> Waiter: 'The usual? The usual? There's no such thing as the usual, sir.'[85]

At the time the cartoon, and the words attached to it, may have had many and various political connotations, but one truth is obvious and self-evident: the Occupation changed everything. Sweets argues that north and south were affected alike:

> War and occupation meant hard times for almost everyone in France. Uncertain employment; shortages of food, clothing, and most consumer goods; restricted mobility; unwelcome regulations and controls from both German occupation authorities and their own government; and other problems contributed to the discontent of most French citizens.[86]

In the end though the goal for most people was a simple one. Kedward states:

> The first expressions of anger in France were at best followed by mute incomprehension. In general the French turned further away from the war and concentrated single-mindedly on day-to-day survival and the search for some return to a semblance of acceptable normality.[87]

Liberation from the conflicts, tensions and divisions of the Occupation came in 1944. However, the ease with which these social, economic and political difficulties were overcome should not be exaggerated.

Larkin highlights this point: 'There was a sense in which everyone who had lived through the Occupation was vicariously under scrutiny. The attitude of the man in the street to Vichy and the Germans during the Occupation had been as much a matter of temperament as of class or political allegiance.'[88]

CHAPTER TWO

Vichy and collaboration

From the National Revolution to Hitler's revolution

> The new order cannot be a servile imitation of foreign experiments
> – though some of these experiments are not without sense and
> beauty. Each people, however, must conceive of a regime suitable
> to its temper and genius. A new order is an absolute necessity for
> France. Our tragedy is that we shall have to carry out in defeat
> the revolution which we were not even able to realise in victory,
> in peace, in an atmosphere of understanding among equal nations.
>
> Marshal Pétain[1]

Vichy is a tranquil, pleasant and unsuspecting town. In geographical
terms it is almost the exact centre of France. It is famous for its spa
water and its genteel way of life, and in the mid-1990s it was being
marketed under the soundbite '*La Ville est une fête*' – a totally ironic
slogan given the wartime history of the place.[2] In 1940 the small
provincial town was the administrative HQ of the pro-German regime
headed by France's most decorated soldier, Marshal Philippe Pétain.[3]
It had been chosen for its convenient geographical location, excellent
communications and ample hotel space. It was, if you like, the French
equivalent of Cheltenham, Harrogate or Tunbridge Wells. However, a
visitor to the town in the early twenty-first century would have to dig
long and hard before unearthing any reference to Vichy's notoriety in
the 1940s. The fact is that today the town is quietly embarrassed about
its wartime infamy.

The reality of the situation is that between 1940 and 1944, the
humble and picturesque town of Vichy was home to conservatives, traditionalists, anti-semites, and even the odd heart-and-soul fascist. It
was the idyllic background against which Pétain and his right-hand

man, Pierre Laval, attempted to govern the southern, unoccupied zone and negotiated with Hitler. When full executive power passed to the aged Marshal on 16 June 1940, he came to be regarded by some as a God-like saviour figure. The writer Paul Claudel was one of the first people to be seduced by the aura of the man:

> Marshal, this poem is about someone coming back to life. It is no small thing, coming back from the dead! . . . Marshal, here is that France in your arms, who has only you and who is coming slowly back to life, slowly and with a low voice . . . Marshal, the dead have a duty and that is to return to the living . . . Lift up your eyes and see something great and tricoloured in the heavens! Something in the heavens for ever, which cannot but prevail. Something which is, of itself, stronger than the darkness – the dawn![4]

So, there was Claudel-like sycophancy; there was also a genuine and most sincere belief that Pétain *was* God:

> Our Father,
> Who art our leader,
> Hallowed be thy name.
> Thy kingdom come.
> Thy will be done
> On earth, so we may live.
> Give us each day our daily bread.
> Give France back her life.
> Let us not fall back into vain dreams and falsehoods.
> But deliver us from evil,
> O Marshal![5]

In time, for some, this image was to consolidate itself; for others it evaporated, and Pétain quickly came to be viewed as a sad and pathetic fool, incapable of governing and totally in the hands of the cold and calculating Laval. Here it is important to note, as Milza and Sirinelli do, that Vichy was not a bloc (as its opponents often claimed) but a 'tower of Babel', 'diverse' and 'pluralistic'.[6] There was a range of ideas and influences at play at Vichy, and anyone wishing to explore and understand the regime has to take this fact on board. It would be more accurate to say that there was, as Birnbaum argues, a 'Vichy of Pétain' and a 'Vichy of Laval'.[7] Nevertheless, a cult rapidly established itself around the Marshal – an idolatry that was enhanced to an astonishing degree by the swathes of propaganda that began to emanate from the apex of the regime. By August 1944, Pétain had been captured by the Germans, and following the Liberation was to be imprisoned for life on the Île d'Yeu, an obscure and isolated island off the west coast of France.[8] Atkin neatly summarises the life and career of Pétain in the headings he chooses for his book chapters: namely, 'The officer, 1856–1914', 'The general, 1914–18', 'The marshal, 1919–39', 'The saviour, 1939–40', 'Le chef, 1940–2', 'The collaborator, 1940–2', 'The figurehead, 1942–3', 'The exile, 1944 . . .' and 'The man and the myth'.[9] As these titles indicate, Pétain had an extraordinary persona. In 1940 he was, at the same time, France's most famous living soldier *and* the man who had led his country into collaboration with Nazi Germany.

This chapter will consider the general political climate at Vichy and the main contours of government; it will then move on to assess the two ultra-controversial *Pétainiste* initiatives of 1940 – the National Revolution and collaboration; and finally it will offer a series of perspectives on the question of how we should interpret the Vichy era as a whole.[10] A number of key historical debates will underpin the chapter: How did the Vichy regime operate and how should it best be understood and characterised? What was the inspiration behind the National Revolution? What factors explain the policy of collaboration? To what extent was France guilty of assisting Nazi Germany in the Holocaust? What was the relationship and interplay between Pétain and Laval, and also between the National Revolution and collaboration? What was the reaction of France and French people to the Vichy regime and Pétain?

On 16 June 1940 Paul Reynaud resigned as premier and was succeeded by Pétain. Six days later, the Marshal signed the Armistice with Germany and on 10 July the National Assembly voted full powers to Pétain. The Third Republic had, in effect, voted itself out of existence. The Armistice allowed for an 'independent' French government in the southern zone and in time this new authority came to be known by a variety of pseudonyms, chief among which were 'the Vichy regime', '*l'État français*' and the 'Vichy administration'. When these terms are used, historians are talking about the same political entity. And, in essence, what we have to understand is that the Vichy regime was sweet revenge for all those conservative and right-wing forces excluded from the Third Republic in its later years[11] – a vehement riposte to the previous regime.

The pace of life at Vichy was slow, relaxed and leisurely – a far cry from the trauma, emotion and devastation of world war. It was as if Vichy was insulated from the rest of France and the rest of the world. Things continued as if nothing untoward had happened: a pleasant setting for, arguably, an overtly unpleasant regime. From the onset, Vichy had all the characteristics of a simple, paternalistic monarchy. Following the 'suicide' of the parliament-dominated Third Republic, Pétain saw no need to return to representative government and acted, to all intents and purposes, like an *ancien régime* sovereign. Goubert, for one, emphasises the fact that the Vichy regime meant the end of the Republic and the end too for parliament and democratic elections.[12] There were ministers and departments – a façade of democratic government – but the fundamental reality was that Vichy was hierarchical, old fashioned and anti-democratic.[13] Pétain did nothing to dispel this notion and actually encouraged it. He began all his official communications: 'We, Philippe Pétain . . .'

The key relationship was that between Vichy and Berlin. At times it was Laval (or whoever else was filling the role of first minister), rather than Pétain, who pulled the diplomatic strings. There is much debate as to the exact nature of the Pétain–Laval relationship; suffice it to say that, in certain periods, Laval was given much room in which to negotiate and barter on behalf of the regime. The view that Pétain was an old man who was quite happy to hand over full power to Laval is clearly too simplistic; the reality was that Pétain involved himself in the things that he wanted to involve himself in, and knew what he wanted to know; and handed power over to Laval on that basis.

The National Revolution

The key development in the early years of Vichy was the National Revolution. It was Pétain's personal policy agenda: a credo, a slogan, a glorified political statement. In essence it was all about the 'hope of regeneration'.[14] Griffin might call the Vichy regime 'para-fascist',[15] but the National Revolution was, over and above everything else, conservative in nature; and framed, primarily, as a retort to what the Marshal and his confidants perceived to be the innate corruption and weakness of the Third Republic. Here the intellectual importance of Maurras is central: Griffiths, Rémond and Larkin all agree that the traditionalist ideas of the Action Française were of profound significance in the development of *Pétainiste* thought.[16] There is an excellent moment in the 1993 film, *Pétain*, when on a very tranquil summer day, soon after France's military defeat, the Marshal and Laval are sitting by the river in Vichy talking about their future plans; Pétain says rather casually that the new regime needs a simple philosophy . . . and within seconds floats the idea of '*travail, famille, patrie*'.[17] Pétain viewed 1940 as a political, rather than a military, defeat; and as such argued that an overtly political response to the collapse of 1940 was required. The National Revolution was thus designed, and viewed, as the perfect antidote to the Third Republic: real values replacing undiluted decadence.

For the historian of the National Revolution there is a plethora of key debates. Who and what were the main influences on Pétain and his conservative philosophy? What were the prime elements of the 'revolution' envisaged by the Marshal? How, and to what extent, was it influenced by Nazism? Was it in essence a 'revolution' or something very different – a 'renovation' or 'restoration' perhaps? How did ordinary French people react to the initiative? And, finally, was it home-grown or imported? There is also a more fundamental question: was the National Revolution, in reality, a political project formulated on the spur of the moment as a response to the crisis and catastrophe of 1940? Or was it, rather, a longstanding *Pétainiste* scheme – a product in effect of the Marshal's own right-wing political agenda – that was instituted cleverly and opportunistically amid the ruin of defeat? This is an important question, for if Pétain's crusade is shown to be planned, and thought out meticulously over decades of political plotting, it must be viewed as a highly ideological development. This in turn would affect our understanding of the whole rationale behind the project and its relationship, or non-relationship, with Nazi ideology.

The National Revolution emerges, in general terms, as an exercise in nostalgia.[18] This is exactly how Pétain envisaged it. His ancient mind was drawn naturally towards France's 'glorious past' and, in a sense, it was predictable that his blueprint for a defeated and crisis-ridden France would mean going 'backwards' rather than 'forwards'. It was also entirely in keeping with the new leader's mindset that all the main influences on him, and his project, should emerge from France's past, rather than its present: Barrès, Maurras and Péguy were three of these. As Anderson has stated: 'The principles, the attitudes and the rancours of the National Revolution were deeply embedded in the French Right.'[19]

In an era of German occupation, German tutelage and German exploitation, there was in fact something peculiarly French about the National Revolution. In other spheres of policy Pétain may have merited being branded a 'traitor' but in, and through, the National Revolution he appeared to make a conscious attempt to return France to her authentic roots: a kind of nostalgic patriotism. This meant that the Vichy regime distinguished overtly between 'French' and 'non-French' elements; hence the *Pétainiste* belief in 'anti-France' – a make-believe coalition of 'threatening' forces (Jews, socialists, foreigners, protestants, freemasons *et al.*).[20] Some will say that the National Revolution was nothing more than 'imported Nazism' but this is to miss the point. There were Nazi traits and influences at work in Pétain's project – how could there not be? – but it is to underestimate the will of the Marshal, and the whole rationale of the 'revolution', to describe it as imported *anything*. Rather, it was a cocktail of Frenchness and indigenous tradition – a project all about '*la vieille France*', as Werth puts it.[21]

The National Revolution was also an innately 'French' scheme in the sense that it was the project of those people in the Vichy administration who stood furthest away from the Germans and who wanted to lift the spirits of France by returning to the essence of French society and French history. So, the hiatus of defeat and collapse offered an ideal opportunity for change and reform. In October 1940 Pétain outlined his thinking:

On this mound of ruins we must now reconstruct France. The new order must not in any sense imply a return, even disguised, to the mistakes that have cost us so much; nor should we look for signs of a sort of 'moral order', or revenge for the events of 1936. The new order must not be a slavish imitation of other people's experiments. Some of these experiments are not without meaning or beauty. But every people should conceive a regime adapted to its climate and its national spirit. The new order is a necessity for France. We must bring about in defeat, tragically, the revolution that in victory, in peace, in voluntary alliance of equal peoples, we were unable to achieve.[22]

Here it is important to note that Laval, the Paris Nazis *and* the German occupiers had little time for the National Revolution. These people viewed it as a parochial and rather strange initiative. While Laval viewed it 'with contempt'[23] – his admiration for Nazism and semi-nostalgia for the Third Republic were always too powerful[24] – the Nazis in Paris ridiculed it as symptomatic of a 'soft' administration, and the Germans displayed both ignorance of, and suspicion towards, it. As Anderson notes, Vichy's authoritarian and retrospective outlook had very little in common with the revolutionary totalitarianism of the Nazis.[25]

Although historians constantly use the phrase National *Revolution*, Pétain tended to prefer the term National *Restoration*. This indicates the real nature of the initiative; as Sirinelli remarks, the 'reactionary' side of the National Revolution was always extremely visible.[26] What Pétain was aiming at was not a 'revolution' in the strict sense of the word – a radical and progressive change – but a return to old values and norms. The different strands in Pétain's thinking are reflected in a passage from his speech of 11 October 1940:

> We must reconstruct. I want to achieve this reconstruction with your support. The Constitution will be the legal expression of a Revolution already begun in fact, for institutions are of value only through the spirit which they embody. A Revolution cannot be made only through laws and decrees. It can be successful only if the nation understands it, and asks for it, if the people accompany the Government along the path of essential renewal.[27]

In a counter-revolutionary vein that was both fundamental and explicit, Vichy attempted to overturn the heritage of 1789 in one fell swoop. Political democracy was blamed for everything; as Rémond declares, 1940 was the revenge of all the forces that had never accepted the Revolution.[28] In trying to do this, it was bound to come across as naïve and cack-handed. In terms of ideas and symbols, it was simple enough to substitute the revolutionary slogan of '*liberté, egalité et fraternité*' with the new (but old) triptych of '*travail, famille, patrie*'; however, in the arena of practical policies it was less sensible to think that a hastily thought-out policy agenda could return France, at a stroke, to an idyllic and over-glorified past. For this reason, Wright labels the Vichy triptych as 'more slogan than reality'.[29] It was also difficult to rationalise and comprehend the Vichy war cry, 'conservative revolution' – a feeling that is enhanced when one realises that there were ever-present tensions between conservatives and modernisers within the corridors of power. However, in a range of spheres, Vichy leaders genuinely believed that they could turn back time: a solidly-built France, constructed on the pillars of age-old values, *could* take the place of a nation erected upon the follies of republicanism and 1789.[30] The underlying message was clear: simple rules and concrete realities should, and would, replace abstract values. In short, this meant that 'common sense' was in, and the French Revolution and the Declaration of the Rights of Man were out.

On economic matters – in the early days at least – Vichy was ultra-conservative. Pétain's conviction was that France would always be 'an essentially agricultural country';[31] he and his associates on the right were convinced that France could be rejuvenated by what was called a 'return to the land'. In this spirit, it was inevitable that peasants and peasantism, and the innate strength associated with these two terms, should be idolised by the administration.[32] Likewise, the regime glorified 'soil' and 'roots', ancient crafts and rural trades, and as if to emphasise its self-identification with the ancient agricultural past, it chose the *francisque* as its primary emblem and letterhead logo.[33] Although in many ways this part of Vichy doctrine overlapped with parts of Nazi ideology, it is fairly clear that 'peasantism' was a creed conceived in France.[34]

In this spirit, Vichy offered special aid packages to small family farms. In the end only 'about a 1,000'[35] people responded to the government's 'return to the land' policy and took advantage of the financial incentives that were offered under the scheme. For the most part, the idea of a renewed, rural nation, administered by a special peasant corporation,[36] had to remain an unfulfilled goal.[37] The idolisation of agrarian France was, however, just one element of the regime's organised nostalgia. Village life was also admired, as was the age-old role of the Catholic Church in small communities. One Vichy poster tried to bring life to this all-round vision. It featured a picture of a typical French village – complete with neatly-mown fields and church. The caption read: 'PATRIE SUIVEZ MOI! GARDEZ VOTRE CONFIANCE EN LA FRANCE ÉTERNELLE'.

Vichy was a regime of contrasts. Rural nostalgia sat side by side with a powerful belief in corporatism. Here perhaps there *was* a genuinely fascist idea, with all economic activity to be monitored by state corporations. In many ways this idea was sold as a 'third way' between capitalism and socialism.[38] Twenty-nine professional 'families' were put in charge of the French economy – one for each industry. A labour charter was also introduced in March 1941. The overall aim, so the Vichy authorities announced, was 'social peace'; or as Griffiths puts it, the prevention of 'class war'.[39] The underlying assertion was that individualism and the class struggle were unhealthy and antiquated concepts; it was argued that what the 'new' France needed more than anything was harmony and reconciliation.[40] The reality though was different. As McMillan argues, corporatism revealed Vichy's desire to smash the unions and the working class, and as Milza and Werth also conclude, Vichy was essentially capitalist whatever the corporatist window-dressing and propaganda might suggest.[41]

Initially, therefore, there was a myriad of influences at Vichy – 'reactionary, monarchist, corporatist, clerical'[42] – but in the end it was the 'modernists' who took sway and the government, whatever Pétain's personal prejudices, began to embrace state planning and technology (the inception of a 10-year plan being a prime example of this policy in action). This development was also a consequence of increased German control in the southern zone and the after-effects of the 1942 invasion. Thereafter, the Germans dominated and Vichy economic thinking had no choice but to adapt itself to the prevailing wind. (Larkin claims that, in 1943, 15 per cent of France's agricultural produce, 40 per cent of her industrial output and 85 per cent of her vehicle production went straight into German hands.[43]) The influence of the 'sharp young things' reached a peak in the period between 1942 and 1944; and in the end, as Rémond notes, the legacy was a positive one for France, with the country's post-war economic planners heavily in debt to the strategists of the late-Vichy period.[44]

It could also be argued that there was a progressive dimension to Vichy rule in the realm of social affairs and welfare.[45] For the most part, however, the regime's attitude to issues like demography and reproduction has been interpreted as traditionalist and reactionary;

Copley argues that 'conservative France wished for a moral revolution'[46] and Pétain was sure that the disaster of 1940 was inextricably linked to the falling French birth-rate – and the knock-on consequence of this for the military effort. More children, he argued, would mean more soldiers, and more soldiers, he surmised rather simplistically, would mean more military victories. This then, for Pétain, was the urgency of the situation and, for us, a graphic illustration of the Marshal's way of thinking.

In power, Pétain prioritised the birth-rate issue and sent a clear message out to the effect that a woman's place was in the home. His regime used both stick and carrot in trying to make this edict a reality.[47] Abortion and contraception were made illegal and all female employment was prohibited in October 1940. To encourage reproduction, family allowances were increased in April 1941, parents who had three or more children were granted special privileges (the mother would acquire a 'priority card'; the father would be allowed to work overtime), and women who rejected offers of paid employment would be paid an average wage to stay at home. Predictably too, homosexuality and pederasty were also vilified.[48] In the end, whatever the success of the policy – and that was debatable – the impression left was of a man and an administration eager to return to a society in which women were valued only for their fertility. This sentiment runs through much of Vichy's propaganda. For instance, the government issued a special poster which stated: '1941 L'ANNÉE DU NETTOYAGE'. The meaning was clear: France had to rid herself of 'unhealthy' influences. However, the key image was of a blonde, bare-footed, cleaning woman tidying up. It was no coincidence that the female in the poster was presented in such a traditional role.[49]

More generally, Pétain glorified the family. As an opening gambit he banned the Declaration of the Rights of Man and Citizen, arguing that 'man' and the 'individual' did not exist except in the abstract. In reality, he argued, it was communities like the family that existed and that deserved praise, attention and rights.[50] He also established a government department – the General Secretariat for Youth and the Family – to monitor developments and make policy in this area. Vichy's social policy had a number of emphases but there was one overall aim: to strengthen the institution of the family. The regime tried to encourage 'enlarged families' – where adults would care for the very young and the very old. It also railed against divorce which in April 1941 was banned in the first three years of marriage. The reactionary nature of Vichy policy was illustrated by the fact that all divorce cases linked to adultery had to be referred to the police.[51]

There were other planks to Vichy's moral crusade. Youth and its virtues were glorified and the regime encouraged an array of almost fascist-style movements for teenagers and young people: the *Chantiers de Jeunesses* and the *Compagnons de France* to name but two.[52] These groups attempted to imbue youngsters with the 'right' attitudes. However, as Milza points out, it is significant that Vichy never created one *single* youth movement – a sign for him that there was no real totalitarian project.[53] Nevertheless, the *idea* of youth was integral to Vichy – despite, or maybe because of, the fact that the regime was personified by an ageing leader. A key Vichy propaganda poster featuring the words, 'FRANCE NOUVELLE' incorporated the phrase 'À NOUS JEUNES'. Significantly too, this poster incorporated the image of two blond, dynamic-looking faces.[54]

The administration was eager to 'clean up' what it viewed as a decadent and corrupt education system and thus determined to help foster a more 'patriotic' climate in schools. The Vichy regime also made a strenuous effort to point out the dangers implicit in alcohol and over-indulgence (this of course harked back to one of the right's initial post-1940 observations: that the Fall of France was more about social indiscipline – alcoholism, for example – than about military failure pure and simple).[55]

In all of its strictures on the family, morality and demography, Vichy knew that it was also tapping into Catholic and Christian teaching. In this sense, it anticipated that it would have a *de facto* ally in the Church. Rémond states that Vichy was 'allied to the Church' and 'invoked its patronage', while Larkin claims that the Church gained 'various tokens of government favour'.[56] Halls also explains how the Germans viewed Pétain's National Revolution as essentially anti-secular; they were, he claims, wary of its 'clericalism' and 'anti-secularity'.[57] For most of the time this was most certainly the case. However, as Atkin and Tallett warn us, the Church never spoke with one single voice; it was a mosaic rather than a monolithic bloc. And on some issues, like marital separation, it is clear that the Church did not always get its own way.[58] In the light of this, it would probably be sensible not to exaggerate the extent of the Church's influence and the strength of the Vichy–Church 'alliance'.[59]

Throughout its policy pronouncements and preaching on morality, there was one underlying theme: the belief that Vichy incarnated some higher kind of patriotism. In sinister propaganda posters individual people were challenged to emulate Pétain's level of patriotic service – '*Êtes-vous plus Français que lui?*'[60] Throughout the Marshal's time as puppet leader of the unoccupied zone, he talked in a passionate way about 'France'. This was done more in spiritual than in territorial terms (as in truth Pétain had to, given the provision in the Armistice which split the nation into 'French' and 'non-French' zones). The Marshal claimed that, in becoming leader of France in the summer of 1940, he had 'sacrificed himself' to the nation in some kind of profound, ultra-noble gesture. He also believed, less than modestly, that he alone personified all the main French virtues.

Although in one sense Pétain's patriotic credentials *were* unquestionable – the 'Victor of Verdun' was France's greatest living soldier – in another, perhaps more important way, it was difficult to comprehend how a man who had agreed to collaborate with Hitler could continue to play the 'patriotic' card. The fact of the matter was that France was divided – not just in a geographical sense (occupied zone/unoccupied zone) but also in social, political and economic terms. In this situation, how *could* Pétain have the arrogance to claim to be patriotic, especially when he was collaborating with and, in some respects, aping fascist ideas? In the end, after the Liberation of France, Pétain was sentenced to death for his treasonous activities during the period of the Occupation, even though he continued to believe that through the National Revolution and other initiatives, he was piloting France back to her essential roots and eternal values.

On the whole, it is difficult to gauge the popularity of the National Revolution with ordinary people living in the southern zone. Perhaps the best that can be said is that it was tolerated. While there was respect for Pétain and his personal history, there was no genuine love – hence the need for massive, and often ridiculous, Vichyite propaganda campaigns to whip up support. There were other problems at the heart of the Marshal's master plan. The speed with which the National Revolution was launched hinted at one of two things: either that it was the natural outcome of Pétain's increasing political involvement in the 1930s – he was a behind-the-scenes plotter in the political crisis of February 1934 – or that it was a spontaneous, and perhaps hasty, response to catastrophe. Lee argues in fact that the only chance 'fascism' had of imposing itself in France was through war and collapse.[61] The National Revolution was never a product of the popular will; rather, just the personal agenda of an aged and perhaps bitter old man – and also, significantly, of a man who never had the political instincts of a Laval. This meant that Pétain was invariably viewed as out of touch, and his political ideas suffered naturally as a result.

There were also the inevitable tensions: on the level of ideas between traditionalists and modernists, on the level of personalities between Pétain and Laval, and on the level of governance between Berlin and Vichy. These frictions often boiled over into confrontations, with negative consequences for practical policy-making. Nonetheless, one is left with the feeling that Pétain did not really care greatly about the practical success of the National Revolution; perhaps all he really wanted to do was to make a statement of belief and to rubbish the hated Republic. With no real time to make its mark, the National Revolution did not leave a massive imprint on French society. Apart from the legacy in terms of state planning – which the Fourth Republic eagerly built upon – there was very little bequeathed to France, except the memory of a rather sad and anachronistic value-system.

Collaboration

If the National Revolution was, in essence, about France returning to its roots and rediscovering its Frenchness, collaboration was, in fundamental terms, about the Vichy regime and ordinary French people kowtowing to a foreign power. If one term has emerged from the wartime period with a horrible, unpleasant stigma attached to it, it is this one. Collaboration, though, is not the most straightforward word to define, nor the easiest phenomenon to identify. It is very much an umbrella term and, as such, it is essential to think of it in the plural. At its narrowest collaboration can be defined as a 'working relationship' at governmental level between victor and vanquished; and at its broadest, as any sign – or even hint – of contact between occupier and occupied. Similarly, the way in which collaboration has been perceived varies widely; in the case of the arch-conspirators at governmental level, or on an ideological plane, it has been viewed as the most heinous of crimes – to be punished with death – while in the context of

ordinary people going about their everyday lives, it has been interpreted as an almost inevitable consequence of the Occupation.

Collaboration came in many forms: liaisons in the black market, personal friendships and, most notorious of all, 'collaboration horizon-
tale'.[62] As Price remarks, it could take the form of calculated behaviour
or just accidental relationships.[63] At its most overt – Defrasne argues
that it reached its 'summit' between June 1941 and December 1942[64]
– collaboration meant partnership at a governmental level between the
Vichy administration and Hitler (or put more accurately, the subservience of France to Germany).[65] The logistics of collaboration were
mentioned initially in the Armistice of 22 June 1940, and confirmed
via the historic Pétain–Hitler handshake at Montoire on 24 October
1940.[66] This handshake was a potent symbol, but thereafter, it was
Laval and Hitler's ambassador in France, Otto Abetz, who played the
pivotal roles in Franco-German relations. It was the former who, with
the tacit approval of Pétain, masterminded one of the most controversial of Vichy's policy initiatives, the STO, and on a level even more
gruesome, the deportation of Jews to Germany.

While it is interesting to debate the ethics and morality of collaboration, it is probably more important to assess how and why it actually took place. Defrasne helps us in this respect. He says that at root
collaboration was the product of 'passion' (sympathy and admiration
for Nazi Germany), 'acceptance' (the notion that some type of 'partnership' was unavoidable given the events of 1940) and 'self-interest'
(the ambition of many French politicians and officials).[67] Each of
these themes is important in trying to understand the essence of
collaboration.

At its most stark, collaboration was a desperate and unavoidable
reaction to defeat and collapse in 1940. There was, it could be argued,
no real alternative. That said, there were other factors at play. In this,
Pétain's behaviour was central. In agreeing to collaborate, the Marshal
believed that he was 'giving' himself to protect France from further
Nazi savagery – the 'shield' that would work in tandem with de
Gaulle's 'sword' (as he was happy to reiterate so frequently). In this
sense Pétain was pursuing a strategy of damage-limitation.

Laval's attitude was different, and on the surface far less 'principled'.
As an ultra-pragmatic politician (Pétain, of course, was first and foremost a military man), he had deduced that the war was a confronta-

tion between fascism and communism and that everyone, including himself, had to make a choice. He opted for Hitler. Collaboration suited his pacifistic outlook and also gave him the chance to jockey for position in a post-Pétain, Hitler-controlled 'new Europe'. Laval's surrender to Nazi Germany was accompanied by a blossoming personal friendship with Abetz, and a growing interest in supporting the German war effort (for example, he offered 200 pilots to Hitler for his air battle with Britain).[68]

Beyond the issue of personalities, there was a longstanding belief in France – evident especially in the 1930s – that an alliance with the diplomatic powers of central Europe was an inevitable, and also desirable, arrangement.[69] Laval, when French foreign minister in the mid-1930s, had been keen to explore the possibility of Franco-Italian and Franco-German understandings. The contours of diplomacy in the second half of 1940 should, therefore, come as no huge surprise.

On the French side, there were other factors encouraging the search for an accommodation with Germany: the desire, or need, to impress the Germans in an effort to water down the main terms of the Armistice and the genuine belief that the Vichy regime and Hitler stood for similar values – the notion, in effect, that collaboration was an ideological understanding. Collaboration can also be interpreted in foreign policy terms. For a start, the British bombardment of the French fleet at Mers-el-Kébir in July 1940 had totally alienated the Vichy leadership and the regime's enthusiasm for collaboration could thus be viewed, quite plausibly, as a determined effort to snub the British and tap into French Anglophobia. Furthermore it was true that Vichy's help would be useful for the Germans' war effort, whether in central Africa, North Africa or Europe itself. One should not exaggerate Hitler's enthusiasm for collaboration. He didn't want a partner, but he did need a servant. Overall it would be wise not to stray too far from Paxton's conclusion; namely, that collaboration was a French proposal, not a German demand.[70]

If the National Revolution was predominantly the project of Pétain, collaboration was – with the acquiescence of the Marshal – the issue on which Laval acquired his main notoriety. In one sense this is ironic, because Laval was not involved in the signing of the Armistice (which first mentioned collaboration), and because for much of the wartime period he was either out of power or, when in power, viewed by the Nazis as a *hindrance* to an effective working relationship between the two countries (or so he seems to claim in his unpublished diary.)[71] Nevertheless, Laval has given observers – at the time and since – plenty of ammunition with which to blacken his name. The first lines of his diary, written while in prison at Fresnes, reflect this fact:

Mr. President,

During my hearing yesterday you handed me the Act of Accusation filed on 13 June 1945, during my absence from France. I wish to thank you for this communication. It has enabled me to know the charges brought against me. They consist in two accusations: first, to have threatened the internal security of the State; second, to have had relations with the enemy in time of war. I hasten to set forth in writing my immediate reactions to this document.[72]

Laval's 'political' co-operation with Nazi Germany may have been the most scrutinised form of Franco-German collaboration but there were, however, other significant 'types'. In the economic sphere collaboration was all-pervading: from grand Laval initiatives like the STO – which involved thousands of French workers being 'loaned' to Germany – to small individual black market deals involving the French and the German occupiers, and other unscrupulous arrangements in between these two extremes. At one point during the war almost half of France's economic resources were being earmarked for the German war effort – significant evidence of the level and scope of economic collaboration.

On a social level, collaboration was unavoidable. In the northern zone, one *had* to comply with German dictates and follow German-devised rules – otherwise there would be trouble. It was also very difficult *not* to communicate with representatives of the occupying force and *not* to patronise commercial establishments either owned or frequented by German officials. In this sense it is problematic to differentiate between what is now labelled 'passive' and 'active' collaboration. Simone de Beauvoir is one high-profile figure to fall foul of post-war commentators; her visits to German-patronised cafés have been interpreted by some as tantamount to collaboration.[73]

Vichy and the Jews

The most notorious aspect of the wartime period was Vichy's attitude, and policy, towards the Jews. As Adler states: 'The anti-Jewish laws established in France in October 1940 marked the beginning of the application by the Germans and Vichy of an anti-Jewish policy that was still in the process of elaboration.'[74] Even though Cobban has argued that France's anti-semitic legislation lagged far behind Hitler's, another commentator, Webster, has described Pétain's policy as akin to 'an inhumane crusade.'[75] Whatever the verdict, it is clear that the Vichy regime was, to a greater or lesser extent, an agent in Hitler's Final Solution, and that is the ignominy which the regime, and its personnel, have had to live with since.

Institutional anti-semitism in France during the wartime period was a mix of Vichy laws and German ordinances (for good measure the occupiers monitored and examined all 'French' legislation).[76] The anti-semitism of Vichy can be viewed from a number of angles. Two can be considered here. First, under the Armistice agreement, Pétain's administration undertook to repatriate all German Jews who had fled to France as refugees in the 1930s – a task that Laval, in particular, carried out ruthlessly in an effort to guarantee that Hitler would actually spare indigenous 'French' Jews. Second, the whole Vichy crusade can be viewed as another sad episode in the long history of French anti-semitism, and also as a graphic reminder of the regime's belief in the existence of a threatening coalition of 'anti-France' forces.[77] Here it is easy – and perhaps, for some, convenient – to add Vichy to the genealogy of right-wing French racism which starts with Drumont and also incorporates Barrès, the anti-Dreyfusards, Maurras, the Action Française and the *ligues*. It is useful to keep these two contrasting perspectives in mind as our discussion of Vichy anti-semitism proceeds.

It is vital to comprehend the scale of Vichy's anti-semitic crusade. Zuccotti states that: 'More than 24 per cent of the Jews in France perished in the Holocaust.'[78] Larkin declares that, overall, 70,000 Jews were deported from France during the wartime period, of which a third were French citizens, and of which only 2,500 survived. Xavier Vallat, Vichy's Commissioner General for Jewish Affairs,[79] claimed after the war that 95 per cent of French Jews survived the Occupation period; a figure, he asserted, that dwarfed the combined figure for the other occupied countries (5.8 per cent). One must not underestimate the scale of a crusade that, to Adler, amounted to the 'politics of expropriation'.[80] The statutes enacted by Vichy were all-encompassing: they delineated, amongst other things, who was Jewish, who could qualify as a French citizen, and how many Jews could be employed in professional sectors such as medicine and law.[81]

The debate which has preoccupied historians has been a simple and important one: What factors, in reality, explain Vichy's anti-semitic policy? Underpinning this debate are other questions: Was Vichy's anti-semitism homegrown or imported? Was it voluntarily or involuntarily put forward? And finally, and fundamentally, how 'guilty' was Pétain and his regime when one assesses the Holocaust as a whole? Did the administration take part, knowingly, in the anti-Jewish offensive?

As regards Vichy's involvement in the Holocaust, an obvious line of thinking is that which emphasises the indigenous nature of anti-semitism in France.[82] This argument is advanced by Wistrich, who talks about 'an autonomous racist tradition'.[83] Here it is almost assumed that the ideas of Drumont, Barrès and Maurras – among others – percolated through into the dogma and ideology of Vichy; the corollary of this is the view which says that the impact of Nazi anti-semitism on Pétain and Laval was minimal and had no definite influence on the regime's policy-making. Historians who follow this line also point out that Vichy's anti-semitic decrees were introduced very hastily in 1940 and 1941[84]; thus, in no way could they be seen as aping Nazi laws. It is argued that Vichy's early legislation actually *pre-dated* the worst of Hitler's and, most definitely therefore, could not have been anything other than a policy made in France and of French parentage. Add to this the fact that several Vichy ministers were renowned for their racist views – Vallat, Louis Darquier de Pellepoix and Charles Mercier du Paty de Clam.[85] So Pétain may not have made great play of his own anti-semitic beliefs prior to 1940 – if he had them at all – but in power he was certainly surrounded by card-carrying racists.

Alternatively, it could be postulated that it was the Catholic tradition in France, rather than the lineage of anti-semitic ideas, that had a significant impact on Pétain. This claim is made by Price who explains Vichy anti-semitism as 'catholic' and 'nationalistic' rather than 'racialist' *per se*.[86] This perspective is tangential to the previous one in that the Catholic Church prior to 1940 was well known for its less than subtle anti-semitic outlook. And in the months immediately following the Fall of France and Pétain's elevation to full executive power, it would be accurate to say that the Catholic Church gave Vichy's racial laws its covert backing, if not its overt support. So, latent prejudice against the Jews, whether of a secular or religious nature, appears to be of obvious, and paramount, importance.

In a similar vein, it is crucial to acknowledge the influence of the Action Française on the Vichy leader. Maurras – the man who patented the idea of 'anti-France' and the notion of the Jews as one of the four main domestic 'threats' – was, throughout the Occupation period, one of the chief intellectual influences on Pétain. It is clear that Cobban agrees to some extent with this line of thinking. He points out that *L'Action française* was one of the few newspapers allowed to publish freely in the southern zone – as if intimating that Maurras and his movement, because of their ideological proximity to the regime, had special privileges granted upon them by Pétain.[87]

It could be argued that Vichy's anti-semitism was in some way aimed at 'impressing' Berlin. This is a theory put forward by Larkin and is based on Vichy's desire for an improved working relationship with the Nazis; perhaps prompted by the desire for more leeway in policy-making.[88] Here, it is noted that Vichy made a point of introducing the occasional policy aimed at external consumption; like, for example, the decree banning Jews from the *département* in which Vichy, the town, was located, or the piece of legislation which stated that all Jews in the unoccupied zone had to advertise themselves with a pinned-on yellow star. Were these 'showcase' policies which aped Nazi initiatives or were they designed to impress Berlin? Both lines of thinking certainly have their adherents.

These of course are all legitimate lines of argument; each perspective has its own merit and validity and each merges and overlaps with others. However, to form a complete picture, it is vital to explore three other major factors: the defeat of 1940 and its implications, the political machinations of Laval, and the demands of Berlin. McMillan makes the point that amid the catastrophe and national humiliation of 1940, it was a natural, if rather unpleasant, reflex for France – and in particular, the Vichy leadership – to search for a suitable scapegoat.[89] As we have already noted, Pétain was quick to identify the politicians of the inter-war years as guilty of leading France into decline and demise. In time – and, significantly, without too much dilly-dallying – he extended this analysis to include the Jews. Price argues that this state-sponsored xenophobia was a predictable reaction to economic depression, political instability and defeat.[90]

It is difficult though to account for Vichy's anti-semitic policy without acknowledging the pivotal role played by Laval. Again there is no reason to believe that Laval was a heart-and-soul anti-semite in the mould of someone like Vallat, say, but it is crucial to realise that Laval, for most of the wartime period, was the middleman in Berlin–Vichy and Vichy–Berlin communication, and thus played a major role in articulating the administration's position on the Jews. And although he strenuously denied all accusations of wrongdoing, it is clear that Laval had his own personal agenda.[91] He was happy, for example, to barter with Hitler in the most unpleasant of terms – sacrificing foreign Jews in an effort to protect French Jews – and also to execute German-inspired policies with vigour and enthusiasm. One must realise that Laval was a career politician, with very few scruples, who viewed the Jews, first and foremost, as useful bargaining chips. A man of significant ambition – and a political operator who was probably thinking five or ten years ahead in all of his wartime calculations – it is also undisputable that Laval had his eye on a key leadership role in Hitler's 'new Europe'. In this sense, it could be argued that Laval used the Jewish question as a launching pad for his own ambitions – unaware of course that he had backed the wrong horse in Hitler and the Nazis.[92] Naturally too Berlin, and its wartime demands, had a substantial impact on Vichy policy. Whether it was the Armistice, and the exigencies inherent in this document, or the STO or, more generally, the Nazi regime's ideological offensive, the Jews were always going to be a key target.[93]

Collaborationism

The other highly distinctive form of collaboration was that which traded in ideas: collaborationism. Here we must turn our gaze towards the group of idealists, intellects and 'Germanophiles'[94] who gathered in Paris to idolise and emulate the Nazi value-system. These people are variously known as 'pro-Nazis', 'French fascists', 'pro-Germans', 'French Nazis', 'Paris collaborationists' and 'Nazi sympathisers'. For our purposes we will label them 'the Paris Nazis' – probably the best, most descriptive term. These cranky and off-beam individuals never constituted a sizeable force; nor did they ever have much serious influence, although a selection of them did enter the 'French' government in January 1944 when the Germans overran the southern zone.

What we are dealing with here is a group of hardcore collaborators – 'The Ideologists':[95] people like Jacques Doriot, Marcel Déat, Robert Brasillach, Pierre Drieu la Rochelle, Louis-Ferdinand Céline, Alphonse de Châteaubriant, Lucien Rebatet, Fernand de Brinon, Jean Luchaire and Joseph Darnand. To a significant degree, they shared a common set of beliefs. They were overtly pro-Nazi and anti-communist and upheld the notion of 'la France allemande';[96] they saw the Occupation as an opportunity for 'national regeneration' along fascist lines – and also for some kind of European solidarity under the aegis of Hitler's Germany; and they exhibited a pathological hatred of Jews. Notwithstanding this 'common agenda', it would be fair to say that there were three distinct groups of ideological collaborators: the 'fugitives from the French Left'[97] (ex-socialists like Doriot and Déat), the 'literary traitors'[98] (fascist writers inspired by Nietzsche like Drieu la Rochelle and Céline) and the 'opportunists' (people like de Brinon, Luchaire and Darnand who were motivated by the possibilities of personal advancement).[99]

The Parisian collaborationists had very little in common with Pétain and Pétainism. Although de Brinon and Darnand personified the link between Paris and Vichy – both held office under Pétain – the Nazis in the capital generally viewed Vichy as 'soft conservatism'. Sirinelli identifies a definite 'tension' in the relationship.[100] The fact remains, however, that the French collaborationists formed a small and fairly insignificant group. But, in a country which has always placed great store on the power of ideas and intellects, these extremists were acknowledged as important players in the drama of the Occupation era – and were thus treated severely at the Liberation, as the case of Brasillach, in particular, demonstrates. Collaborationism was voluntary, wholehearted and fanatical:[101] this was its uniqueness when compared to other types of collaboration, which were fundamentally involuntary and *forced on* people.

The conclusion must be that collaboration – if defined in its broadest sense – was always going to be inevitable once France had collapsed and had been occupied. It could be argued that collaboration in the corridors of power was the most explicit form of Franco-German 'union', while collaboration in ideas was, possibly, the most demonised. The reality of the situation, also, was that ordinary people, in their everyday lives, would always come into contact with the occupiers – on an economic or social level – and would always, therefore, be accused of collaboration.

The defeat in 1940 had profound implications: on the one hand, the ultra-traditional crusade that was the National Revolution; on the other, the *realpolitik* of collaboration. Historians will forever debate the exact political orientation of Vichy but the truth, as Anderson notes, is that the National Revolution was 'not a coherent unity'.[102] Milza argues that the *Pétainiste* regime shared common ground with that of Salazar and that of Mussolini,[103] but we must remember that the authentic fascists Vichy came into contact with – the Nazis in Berlin and the collaborationists in Paris – had nothing but scorn for the regime's 'soft' ideology. In the end it is hard not to agree with Rémond's assessment of Vichy: 'It was a conservatism triumphant, reaction in its pure state, a mixture of paternalism, clericalism, moralism, militarism and boy scoutism . . . a tragic and ludicrous parody of fascism.'[104]

Lest we forget, Vichy, for most of the wartime period, had little real independence. In the first two years it was, to all intents and purposes, a puppet regime, owing its very existence to one particular article in the Nazi-imposed Armistice. And in the last two years of the war, after the German invasion of the south, its sovereignty had been cut down to virtually nil. Perhaps the best way to interpret Vichy is as a rearguard action: a staunch effort, led by Pétain, to protect what he regarded as French. In this circle too was Laval – pragmatic, cynical and ambitious, and a man who wished to ingratiate himself with the Germans. By the end of 1945 both men had been sentenced: one to life imprisonment and the other to death.

CHAPTER THREE

Resistance

Internal and external

> Speaking in full knowledge of the facts, I ask you to believe me
> when I say that the cause of France is not lost.
>
> De Gaulle[1]

'The Resistance', as a phrase, is a misnomer. There was not *one*, *singular* 'resistance'; rather, and far more accurately, there were thousands of 'resistances', *plural*. This is just one of the myths surrounding the history of the Resistance that needs to be considered – and dispelled. Another is that the Resistance equated, simply, to de Gaulle.[2] This is an entirely false contention – the Resistance was, and still is, a difficult and complex phenomenon to try to understand. Resistance activity was secretive and sometimes mysterious; hence, historians have often been thwarted in their efforts to locate, and comprehend, the true nature and essence of the French resistance.

At root there is one basic question: What actually counted as an act of resistance? The truth is that every resister had his or her own particular way of resisting. From jostling Germans in the street to full-scale sabotage, from non-communication with the occupiers to international military plotting, and from making an ostentatious show of the colours red, white and blue to guerrilla warfare, there were a whole host of different tactics.[3] And in answer to the preliminary question, an act of resistance was, basically, anything that, in the mind of the person or group executing the act, *felt* like an act of resistance.

This chapter will introduce, explain and analyse the phenomenon of resistance. The spotlight will move from the different types of resistance to the nature, make-up and ideology of resistance forces, the problems and obstacles that they faced and, finally, the question of success and achievement.

What was the French Resistance?

There are two key issues. First: what was the 'story' of the Resistance? And second: what *was* the Resistance? It is straightforward enough to sketch out the history of the Resistance. The Germans entered Paris on 14 June 1940 and four days later de Gaulle, broadcasting from London, uttered his famous words about the 'flame of French resistance'.[4] In the 12 months following there were various signs of resistance activity including, most notably, a student protest in Paris, a miners' strike in north-east France, and the birth of several anti-German newspapers. Bédarida argues that the Resistance had 'more sympathisers than activists' in 1940.[5] By 1941 the communists had joined the struggle and in 1942 the Secret Army – the name given to an amalgam of internal resistance militias – was formed. In 1943 the Maquis emerged as an important, and anarchic, terroristic force in the southern zone. Throughout that year efforts were made to unify the disparate anti-German, anti-Vichy forces by the formation of the MUR (*Mouvements Unis de la Résistance*) in January, the CNR (*Conseil National de la Résistance*) in May, and the CFLN (*Comité Français de Libération Nationale*) in June. None were totally successful, but the de Gaulle-led CFLN emerged as a kind of government-in-waiting. Dreyfus in his history of the Resistance suggests that the various efforts at unification amounted to '*le grand tournant*'.[6] By the end of 1943, and throughout 1944, 'mini-liberations' were taking place all over France and by 26 August 1944 de Gaulle had entered Paris.[7] By 23 October 1944 de Gaulle's *Gouvernement Provisoire de la Républic Française* (GPRF) had been recognised by the Allies. This was the Resistance story in brief.

What was the Resistance? Important clues to its identity may be found in the things that provoked people into resistance: patriotism, morality, instinct, revenge, the onward march of the German war machine.[8] As to the general character of the Resistance, Kedward argues that if one was asked to illustrate the quintessential nature of the Resistance – its mindset and psyche – it would be more appropriate to quote a piece of evocative Resistance poetry than to refer to a political treatise.[9] This is significant: the Resistance is depicted as a phenomenon that was only partly political. Overall, it was the search for an 'ideal, mythical' France rather than any particular sort of political solution or new constitutional framework.[10] For Shennan the phenomenon was, in essence, 'moral' rather than 'political' and based first and foremost on a 'patriotic reflex';[11] for Lévy it was 'very largely spontaneous';[12] while for Ousby resistance was characterised primarily by a special 'language' and 'rhetoric'.[13]

It could also be argued that 'community', or rather 'sense of community', was a vitally important part of the Resistance value-system.[14] Hawes might argue that resistance was the 'individual solution'[15] – and it is certainly true that the Resistance was comprised of individual men and women who had made their own personal 'choice' – but we should not forget that the Resistance was also a shared vision. There were, obviously, frictions and divisions, but fundamentally it remained an alliance or coalition that, at times, developed into a genuine 'community'. And, significantly, this was as true *after* the war as it was *during* it – with veterans associations and the like ensuring that the torch of the Resistance remained alight in the post-war years.[16]

The 'ideology' of the Resistance – where it is possible to identify one at all – was only loose and fragmentary. In some places there was belief in 'republicanism'; in others 'revolution'. As Cady says though, there was 'no one monolithic Resistance discourse'.[17] A general assumption has emerged to the effect that resistance values were of the left.[18] It is difficult to argue with this assertion but there is also another view which says that, in reality, resistance values were not, actually, the converse of those of Vichy. This latter view stresses how the Resistance and Vichy embraced notions of authority, liberty and anti-parliamentarianism.[19] This, obviously, is a contentious line of thinking. So is the argument put forward by Werth which claims that the motives of resisters were not always 'pure'. He speculates that many people in the Resistance were 'scared' – and not particularly imbued with altruistic principles.[20]

The Resistance was, in addition, about justice. In the early days it was about the right of French people to assert their self-determination and to take part in a fight for the survival of their country. Later it evolved into the quest for liberation – or, rather, the quest for a French-sponsored, and not an American-sponsored, liberation. By the end of the conflict it was about the settling of scores, about ad-hoc 'justice' and about locating, and then dealing with, a suitable number of scapegoats. 'A shot. Justice is done': this is how Lottman describes the process.[21]

So, 'complex, confused, under-explored and unexplorable',[22] the Resistance is an intriguing phenomenon. It was a community, yes, but also, at the same time, a socio-political movement with mystical and spiritual overtones. Resisters came from all walks of life, they acted on different motivations and they originated from both north and south of the German-imposed zonal divide.[23] The overall verdict must be that the Resistance was a 'diffused and inchoate phenomenon' which represented 'a remarkable political and social mixture'.[24] There was incredible heterogeneity but, as Hawes points out, all ideological differences were to be put to one side until liberation was achieved.[25]

Varieties of resistance

It could be argued that there were as many types of resistance as there were individual resisters.[26] Generally though, it is agreed that the most obvious sub-division occurs between 'external' and 'internal' resistance or between 'The Resistance of the Interior and the men of London'.[27] These two types are the most clear-cut and the types that will concern us for the greater part of this chapter. There are, however, other ways of thinking about resistance. For a start, one can differentiate between 'active' and 'passive' resistance. This distinction relates to strategy. One was overtly violent and 'heroic', embodied by movements like Free France and the Maquis.[28] The other was altogether more personal and subtle. This form was described in *La Silence de la Mer*, one of the most important pieces of resistance literature.[29] A German officer is billeted to live with a French couple – an uncle and his niece – but, as a mark of protest, the French people make a concerted effort not to communicate with him. The uncle, as narrator, states: 'The silence was unbroken, it grew closer and closer like the morning mist; it was thick and motionless. The immobility of my niece, and for that matter my own, made it even heavier, turned it to lead.'[30]

On another level, it is possible to distinguish between the attitude of individuals and organisations.[31] Take the case of the Catholic Church and the Communist Party. With each there was a 'corporate' line; the reality though was that individuals within each organisation had enough freedom, on occasions, to act unilaterally and disavow the 'agreed line' (there are, for example, numerous documented instances of individual Catholics sheltering Jews).[32]

Moving on, it is also clear that ordinary women – on their own and also as part of groups – played a significant role in the Resistance.[33] Not for nothing is the Resistance, as a movement, often represented as a female or in female terms.[34] Collins Weitz argues that women resisted in lots of different ways, not just in routine tasks, and claims that their general 'self-effacement' is the prime reason why their contribution to the Resistance has always been underestimated.[35] Cady also states that women were at the heart of the 'everyday battle'.[36]

The 'everyday battle' also consumed, and provoked, others. There was assassination and sabotage and direct action.[37] There was also a typical lifestyle:

[Being in the Resistance] demanded a particular psychological balance, which did not come naturally, to remain calm and apparently unconcerned while being continually on the look-out for the black Citröens and green fedoras favoured by the Gestapo. Nor were these all the security precautions required of a full-time *résistant*. Frenay [a Resistance leader] listed all the other habits which experience taught him to adopt: using not one but several *noms de guerre* . . .; carrying false identity papers and being ready to maintain his false identity if he were interrogated; constantly changing the places where he met fellow-*résistants*, forever checking to see if he was being followed and being ready to put on an overcoat or abandon a hat to alter the silhouette he presented; and keeping bolt-holes and retreats known only to himself.[38]

There was less 'heroic' behaviour too. Small, symbolic acts were commonplace: like jostling Germans in the street or passing on false and misleading directions to members of the occupying force. 'Correct' anti-German etiquette was actually formalised in *Conseils à l'occupé*, a special handbook of 'ways to behave' collated by Jean Texcier.[39] Resistance, of a highly-committed type, also took place in a range of varying social spheres: including intelligence, academia, art, and literature.[40]

It should also be noted that resistance was very much conditional on geography. Clearly, in the northern zone, the German occupiers were the conspicuous enemy. In the unoccupied zone though – as Kedward notes – the forces of resistance identified other enemies: capitalists, clerics, anti-semites, police, state unionists.[41] All of these people, to a greater or lesser extent, were closely associated with the regime of Pétain. Nevertheless, the fact remains that resistance was chameleon-like in its persona and its antagonisms. First and foremost, the Resistance was anti-German and anti-Vichy, but it also exhibited a multitude of related animosities.[42]

So, the most obvious characteristic of the Resistance was its diversity. This, as Ousby notes, was possibly its greatest weakness and its greatest strength.[43] The Resistance boasted a particularly mixed social base. Andrieu's research suggests that artisans, small businessmen and students dominated the *Franc-Tireur* organisation, while employees were over-represented in the ranks of *Libération-Sud*.[44] Lévy meanwhile argues that the Resistance was primarily 'working class' and 'republican'.[45] Cole, however, concludes that all social classes were represented at the heart of the Resistance and he reminds us that six members of the wealthy du Granrut family ended up in concentration camps.[46]

External resistance

The external resistance is, of course, the most celebrated form of resistance. The phrase relates to all those resisters who operated from outside France and, most famously, the type of anti-German, anti-Vichy activity associated with de Gaulle and 'the Free French epic', as Werth calls it.[47] We must remember too that de Gaulle encouraged the growth of 'support groups' all over the world.[48] De Gaulle was crucial to the Resistance, but we should not overestimate his importance. In this vein Lévy argues that the Free French leader was only a 'stimulus': the people of France, he suggests, would have reacted anyway.[49]

Even as late as May 1940, de Gaulle was an important figure in the French government, liaising with Reynaud and advancing his own personal views about France's proposed military strategy.[50] He left France days before the Armistice and on 18 June, in his 'prophetic'[51] radio broadcast, stated: 'The flame of resistance must not die.'[52] For this, de Gaulle was disciplined (*in absentia*) for desertion by the army. Nevertheless it was the first signal that a group of French people were ready to fight back.[53] As de Gaulle wrote later:

> I thought, in fact, that it would be the end of honour, unity and independence if it were to be admitted that, in this world war, only France had capitulated and that she had let the matter rest there. For in that case, whatever might be the issue of the conflict – whether the country, after decisive defeat, would one day be rid of the invader by foreign arms, or would remain enslaved – her self-disgust and the disgust she would inspire in others would poison her soul and her life for many generations.[54]

The crusade would achieve its objective on 26 August 1944 when de Gaulle himself strolled down a liberated Champs d'Elysées as the new 'republican monarch'.[55]

Throughout this four-year period, de Gaulle did not endear himself to others. He did not get on with the Allied leaders. Churchill and Roosevelt both viewed him as an arrogant upstart – and he was continually at odds with both. Even so, he was extremely effective in spreading the Free France message across the globe. In his memoirs, de Gaulle wrote:

> At the age of forty-nine I was entering upon adventure, like a man thrown by fate outside all terms of reference. It was nonetheless my duty, while taking the first steps in this unprecedented career, to make sure that no authority better qualified than mine was willing to step forward to bring France and the Empire back into the struggle . . . At this moment, the worst in her history, it was for me to assume the burden of France. But there is no France without a sword. To set up a fighting force was more important than anything. I began work on that at once.[56]

De Gaulle was thus both forceful and vain in his initial diagnosis of France's problems and his future role. As Hartley has argued: 'The aim was to restore the independence and greatness of France; the means to this end would be a growing revulsion on the part of the French people at the shameful conditions of the armistice and an ever-increasing measure of resistance to German domination.'[57]

In essence, as Shennan argues, there were two main phases to the history of the external resistance.[58] The years 1940–42 can be termed the 'London era', with the Free France group based in the English capital.[59] In this period de Gaulle viewed his movement as an 'alternative France'. After the liberation of Algiers in 1942, de Gaulle moved to North Africa and posed as France's leader-in-waiting: thus began the second phase of de Gaulle's wartime activity.[60] Significantly, de Gaulle's Algiers-based 'provisional government' – which 'existed' between May 1943 and March 1944 – included two communist representatives. This was an extremely significant development: de Gaulle had bitten the bullet and, in the interests of resistance unity (and, possibly, much against his will), realised the need for a policy of inclusion.

Many books have been written about de Gaulle: his life, career and political philosophy.[61] It is important for us to grasp some basic points about his personality and his political role. For a start, we must realise that between 1940 and 1944 de Gaulle underwent two important evolutions. First, it is clear that he started the war as a soldier, but finished it as a politician. This was a vital and necessary change that emphasised how far de Gaulle had travelled, career-wise, in four years. Suddenly he was having to adapt to the realities of political life and the demands that this made on him (although his military background continued to condition his political attitudes and behaviour for the rest of his life).

Second, it would be fair to say that, as the war went on, de Gaulle's politics changed. In 1940, as one would expect of a career soldier, de Gaulle was a conservative; one might even describe him as an authoritarian, an anti-republican and a reactionary. By 1944, however, a significant radicalisation had taken place in his attitudes; and in his speeches and writings there was much more talk of change and a 'new republic'. Jackson's analysis shows that the tone of de Gaulle's speeches began to change in 1942. Prior to this date his speeches rarely contained words like 'democracy' and 'republic'; they were politically 'neutral' and aimed at gaining the widest possible support. Jackson claims though that after this date, de Gaulle's speeches became more radical, as if adapting to the changed political circumstances and the urgent need to get left-wing groups 'on board'.[62] Throughout, though, de Gaulle's wartime rhetoric was infected by 'a style of intransigent nationalism'.[63]

These two illustrations indicate how tactically aware de Gaulle had to be. He knew that he had to enter the realm of politics; he knew also that he had to adapt his message to gain maximum support. The corollary was that, in organisational terms, de Gaulle realised the need for unity and coordination between external and internal forces. For various reasons he had no love for the France-based resistance groups, but his realism and political awareness suggested to him that external–internal solidarity was, possibly, the vital prerequisite for liberation. It was as a result of this belief that de Gaulle sent Jean Moulin to mainland France as his personal ambassador. Moulin's mission was simple: to unify the external and internal forces. This he helped to achieve with the formation of the *Conseil National de la Résistance* (CNR) in May 1943.

Appropriate tactics were also crucial in other areas. De Gaulle's initial supposition was that the war would evolve into a world conflict involving Britain, the US and perhaps even the USSR. This was a different line of thinking to that advanced by Laval, whose basic assumption was that Germany would win the war. In the end, Laval was proved wrong and de Gaulle proved right. It is important to note that de Gaulle had a definite strategy; and that was to widen and broaden out the conflict. He actively wished for a world war rather than a more localised conflict: the Resistance, he argued, should think long-term and not just settle for a policy of killing Germans in the short-term.[64] In a similar vein, de Gaulle knew that the French Empire could be very useful to him. It was still 'France', and it was not totally loyal to the Vichy regime, and thus, had much potential.

It is also possible to identify other features of the political de Gaulle. It is clear first that, by nature, he was an autocrat. Of course he had close associates, who formed a small clique around him,[65] but for the most part he was a dogmatic and fairly uncompromising leader; hence his many fall-outs with Allied leaders. It must also be said that he was a good and effective communicator – he specialised in high-sounding speeches and undercover radio broadcasts – and that there was something particularly vain and arrogant about his whole persona. In his war memoirs, for example, he talks continuously in the third person: a sure sign of self-importance.[66]

Second, the notion of 'legitimacy' must be considered. This word was 'of some importance in the Gaullist vocabulary . . . In the eyes of de Gaulle and his adherents they themselves were the true heirs to France's past – an inheritance forfeited by the Vichy government from the moment of Pétain's demand for an armistice.'[67] So, while the Marshal was struggling to assert his credibility, and desperately seeking international diplomatic 'approval', the General was almost *assuming* that his movement had all the necessary legitimacy. He actually seemed to take it as read that his Free France movement *was* France; and also that his 'provisional government' would just walk into power when Germany was defeated. Bédarida actually claims that, in time, de Gaulle came to personify a 'double legitimacy': via the CNR he acquired both political *and* national credibility.[68] For most of the time, there was an arrogance and belief that was, on the one hand, unattractive to onlookers *but*, on the other, hugely necessary to the overall success of the Resistance effort.[69]

And it is in this sense that one must acknowledge the element of destiny and prophecy inherent in de Gaulle's posturings. This is an extremely significant theme. Shennan argues that de Gaulle was a symbol of hope,[70] but more than that perhaps, he viewed himself as *the* man of destiny. Of course he needed the help of others, and of course it made him unpopular, but it could be argued strongly that France urgently required a figurehead and talisman in a period of despondency and severe dislocation.

Internal resistance

The internal resistance, by contrast, was a more complicated and heterogeneous phenomenon. 'Internal resistance' is an umbrella term used to describe the collection of resistance groups operating from within France – whether in the occupied or unoccupied zone. The internal forces were, on the whole, far more anarchic, unorganised and faction-ridden than those operating from abroad. Furthermore, there was a distinctive left-wing character to most of the France-based groups.

It would be true to say that the internal resistance had a different personality north and south of the German-imposed 'border'. In the occupied zone it was anti-German first and foremost. There were several key groups: *Libération-Nord*, *l'Organisation Civile et Militaire* and *Front National*.[71]

In the unoccupied zone resistance forces were up against the ultra-conservative regime of Pétain and, thus, they developed a much more overtly left-wing programme, implicit in which was the belief that radical political change was desirable post-Liberation. In the south there were a host of important groups: *Combat*, *Libération-Sud*,[72] and *Franc-Tireur*.[73] There were other groups of note – *Libérer et fédérer*, *Témoignage chrétien*, the Christian Democrats – but it was *Combat*, *Libération-Sud* and *Franc-Tireur* which had the highest profiles in the south.[74]

Overall, we must acknowledge the massive diversity and serious incoherency of the France-based resistance groups. Larkin dwells on the unorthodox alliances that developed – among Catholics, communists and Gaullists, for example. It was this lack of unity that provoked several efforts at unification. In September 1942 the various military wings of the internal resistance groups were united under the aegis of the Secret Army; the MUR, meanwhile, attempted to unite northern and southern organisations, and received money and arms from London for its pains; and the CNR, established in May 1943, was particularly important because it encouraged Gaullists and communists to work together and was, as a result, recognised by Moscow – a crucial development.[75]

In time, the fragmentary nature of the internal forces became less of an issue. Important efforts were made to increase the coherency, and thus the effectiveness, of the internal resistance and it is true that as the Communist Party and the Maquis came to dominate the anti-German, anti-Vichy crusade, the elements of division could be seen to be of less significance. Eventually the Communist Party and the Maquis did emerge as the two leading groups within the French resistance. They operated independently, and were actually quite suspicious of each other, but in reality they had much in common. Eventually they came together in the *Franc-Tireurs et Partisans Français*.[76]

The Communist Party had been a growing influence in France during the inter-war years. As a political formation it had been an integral part of the 1936 Popular Front government, but it was still relatively small by European standards (it had 72 deputies in 1936). The story of the communists during the war is one of compromises, ambiguity and profound political and ethical dilemmas. The first point to make is that the political activity of the *Parti Communiste Français* (PCF) was seriously compromised for the duration of the bizarre Nazi–Soviet pact of 24 August 1939. This Berlin–Moscow alliance meant that all communist parties in Europe had to stay 'neutral' and were forbidden from mounting any resistance activity at all. Indeed, in France – as elsewhere – the Communist Party, and its newspaper, *L'Humanité*, were actually banned on account of their ultra-pragmatic alliance with Hitler.[77]

The Nazi–Soviet pact may have been comprehensible when viewed in the most Machiavellian of terms – the USSR was not ready to fight; Germany wanted to carve up Poland with its new 'ally' – but for communist parties around Europe (particularly the one in France) it gave rise to a massive moral and political conundrum. The PCF leadership rationalised the Berlin–Moscow understanding as 'a peace pact' but, as Cobban notes, the Communist Party eventually came to be portrayed as a 'tacit ally' of the Nazis.[78] Throughout the inter-war years the PCF had been at the vanguard of the anti-fascist struggle, particularly in 1934 and during the Popular Front years; thus, the 1939 alliance tossed it into 'utter confusion'.[79] There was something quite tragic and psychologically traumatic about the political situation into which the Soviets' alliance with Hitler had thrust their French brethren. Even so, many rank-and-file communists chose to ignore the political implications of the pact and *did* actually resist in the years 1939, 1940 and 1941. Knight cites a communist tract published on 10 July 1940: 'The great hopes of national liberation lie in the people alone. It is only around the working class, with its confidence and courage, that a front can be built, for freedom, independence and national renaissance.'[80] This is clear evidence of individual French communists' *real* attitude in the early period of the war. It remained a very serious offence for PCF members to go against the Moscow-imposed political line, but 'illegal and dispersed as they were',[81] they still played a part in the anti-Nazi struggle.

Everything changed though with the Nazis' invasion of the USSR in 1941.[82] This military initiative suddenly 'freed' communists across Europe from their unpleasant political dilemma; Germany was now the foe and PCF members could now act in line with their consciences. The 1941 invasion allowed French communists to regain their 'patriotic reputation';[83] not only this, but the movement swiftly evolved into the most influential resistance group. As a well organised and highly disciplined political party, the PCF already boasted a powerful underground network and so, in many ways, the party and its infrastructure was a huge asset for the internal resistance.

It could be argued that, during the years 1941–44, the communists became the fulcrum of the Resistance. The Germans and the Vichy authorities certainly viewed them as the most potent resistance group and, as a result of this contention, labelled them 'bandits' and 'terrorists'. In the second half of the war, eight Central Committee members were shot dead by the Germans and half the staff on the party paper, *L'Humanité*, were also killed. This shows that the Germans took the PCF extremely seriously as a resistance force.

And for its part, and perhaps quite naturally, the Communist Party attempted to exaggerate its role. It tried to acquire all the key resistance posts and talked continually about 'martyrs' and the 'revolutionary hope' enshrined by the Resistance and, eventually they believed, by the Liberation. It also involved itself in some of the most unlikely of 'alliances' – with Catholics during the war and with Gaullists after it. So, in tandem with ideological principle, there was also genuine pragmatism.[84] There was also an overtly intellectual strain to the communists' rhetoric; a really powerful belief that the PCF's resistance could and should be viewed as part of the heroic French revolutionary tradition.[85]

The Maquis on the other hand was an anarchic guerrilla-style movement which operated out of the south and was famed, primarily, for its unorthodox and often badly organised terror gangs. For Kedward it was an 'alternative culture' with an 'unorthodox nature and revolutionary potential', while for McMillan it was 'the most dynamic element of the Secret Army'.[86] The most important thing that can be said about the Maquis is that, 60 years after the war, it is still a remarkably under-researched phenomenon and, thus, still difficult to understand fully.[87] It was a part of Frenay's Secret Army, but beyond this there is not a lot of definite information, bar some quite general assumptions. It is Kedward who sums things up best. He writes that the history of the Maquis is 'varied, diffuse . . . inpenetrable, opaque, secret at best, fictional at worst'.[88]

These qualifications are certainly necessary, but it is possible to sketch out some of the main characteristics of the Maquis. In French the word *maquis* means, 'scrub, bush', a definition which is both helpful and unhelpful. It does not define the word and the movement in terms that we would easily understand, but it does hint at one important feature of the phenomenon: its background and location.[89] Indeed, the first thing that should be understood about the Maquis is that it was based in the rural south and actually exploited the mountainous and forested landscape of this region to its advantage. If most resistance forces based themselves in the towns and cities of France, the Maquis – comprised to a large extent of peasants – made a positive virtue out of its fairly disorganised and secretive existence in the woods and valleys of the south. And, if the maquisards did not know what they were going to do next, the Vichy authorities and the Germans certainly would not be able to track or pre-empt their movements. This brilliant unpredictability and spontaneity was, without doubt, the most obvious characteristic of the Maquis.

The Maquis was loosely organised, strong in rural areas, and southern-based.[90] As to the total number of maquisards in France, there have been a whole array of estimates, ranging from 20–30,000 to 140–150,000. What we know with more accuracy is that maquisards grouped themselves together in small units to form a kind of elite, irregular army which specialised in sabotage – cutting railway lines and blowing up bridges. The best insight into the nature of the movement comes via a contemporary recruiting pamphlet cited by Ousby. It announces:

> Men who come to the Maquis to fight live badly, in precarious fashion, with food hard to find. They will be absolutely cut off from their families for the duration; the enemy does not apply the rules of war to them; they cannot be assured any pay; every effort will be made to help their families but it is impossible to give any guarantee in this matter; all correspondence is forbidden. Bring two shirts, two pairs of underpants, two pairs of woollen socks, a light sweater, a woollen blanket, an extra pair of shoes, shoelaces, needles, thread, buttons, safety pins, soap, a canteen, a knife and fork, a torch, a compass, a weapon if possible, and also a sleeping bag if possible. Wear a warm suit, a beret, a raincoat, a good pair of hobnailed boots.[91]

There was no typical maquisard. Often he was a peasant or a communist or even a foreign mercenary. It is fairly clear too, as Kedward notes, that there were two main types of guerrilla fighter: on the one hand, the genuine, principled maquisard; and on the other, the STO runaway caught in the crossfire of war who preferred the dangerous and unpredictable life of an anti-German terrorist to the hard labour of life in a Nazi work camp.[92] Burrin, for his part, contrasts the courage of the early maquisard with the pragmatism of the later 'runaways'.[93]

In this sense, therefore, we should not overestimate the ideological commitment of the Maquis, because for many people it was, solely, a refuge from other less pleasant existences – primarily, working in Germany for the Nazis.[94]

It would be accurate to assert, in addition, that the Maquis operated as a separate entity – though always unpredictable – for no more than two and a half years. Groupings of maquisards appeared from 1942 onwards. By 1944 they were forming 'free republics', but they had also thrown in their lot with the *Forces Françaises de l'Intérieur* (FFI): an umbrella organisation which had regularised, and grouped together, a plethora of irregular military groups – the communist *Francs-Tireurs et Partisans Français* (FTPF), the secret armies and the Maquis – in the hope of masterminding a (relatively) smooth liberation process.

The way in which the Maquis was viewed 'from outside' is also interesting. Vichy and the German occupiers looked upon the maquisard forces as a dangerous irritant: they were 'murderers', 'bandits' and 'outlaws' and they were treated almost like Jews. The British and the Americans, on the other hand, were largely favourable and sympathetic to the Maquis. They armed the rural guerrilla forces with arms and money and, perhaps, felt more comfortable dealing with them than with the communists (generally viewed by the Allies as an overtly ideological and revolutionary element). The regular military forces within France also had very little truck with the maquisards: they were viewed, simply, as amateurish and unorganised.[95] This impression was to gain ground through the wartime years and the Liberation period as the forces of the internal resistance started to dispense their own brand of 'justice'.[96]

Thus, although the Maquis and the other internal resistance groups had the same enemies, and also shared some common beliefs, they were quite distinct as resistance forces. The obvious difference related to ideology; the Communist Party could never totally trust a movement (in the loose sense of the word) which did not share all elements of its dogma and ideology. So, there was always going to be a problem about political labels and tactics: many 'professional' military elements within the resistance 'coalition' were horrified and alienated by the 'criminal' and 'anarchic' behaviour of the maquisards. Bédarida talks about 'insurmountable problems'.[97]

Initially, de Gaulle's Free France grouping and the various movements of the internal resistance had very little in common in terms of tactics, organisation, ideology or expectations at the Liberation. Larkin claims that the internal forces had a 'tenuous relationship' with de Gaulle, but that this improved as a result of Moulin's strategic mission to France.[98] De Gaulle, anyway, had very little time for political parties and their specific agendas; he felt that intra-French division at the end of the war could actually benefit the US and enable the Allies to impose their will at the Liberation. So, basically, de Gaulle just wanted to manoeuvre the internal resistance as he wished; it could be useful to him, but only so long as it acquiesced to his leadership.[99]

There was also a lack of understanding between internal and external forces. The internal groupings were extremely critical of those who had left France; this was viewed, somehow, as the easy option; and as a result, members of the Free France movement were viewed as 'cowards' and 'deserters'. The external forces, meanwhile, were suspicious of the radicalism and political ideology of the France-based groups. De Gaulle was not only wary of left-wing ideas but tended to believe that he alone personified the anti-Vichy, anti-German crusade.

The truth is that in 1940 and 1941 there was a chasm separating the outlook of the internal groupings and that of the external elements – so much so that many people talked of the Free French/Fighting French as if they were in some way separate from the 'Resistance' (which they tended to equate to the internal resistance).[100] Bédarida says that internal and external forces trod 'divergent paths': they were both motivated by the same fundamental conviction (that France was 'eternal') but differed in the way they conceived of the 'struggle' (de Gaulle believed in 'classical military conflict', whereas the France-based groups attached themselves to notions of 'underground action and guerrilla conflict'.)[101] The groups operating from within France also exhibited a powerful republicanism that often evolved into a belief in socialism and a desire for social revolution. As a conservative, de Gaulle found it hard to come to terms with this ideology. By 1942, however, he was embracing 'revolutionary' ideas – at least in his rhetoric – and by May 1943 he had helped to establish the CNR. And by 1944, the communists had come in from the cold. As Jackson says: 'Securing communist support was a vital part of de Gaulle's strategy.'[102] So, by the end of the wartime period, necessity and the force of circumstance had brought external and internal forces into an alliance of sorts; unity and shared purpose was never very strong, but it was just strong enough to enable France to emerge out of the trauma of the Occupation.

Problems and obstacles

If one serious issue for the Resistance was 'unification',[103] the other fundamental problem was its relationship with the Allies. It must be remembered that, during the wartime period, de Gaulle was in exile; he was in a desperate situation and relied for much of the time on the goodwill of his hosts, the British. He also tried to exploit the goodwill of the US but, in a rather rude and unappealing manner, seemed to *assume* that the Allies would help 'rescue' France. This was a big mistake.

The fact of the matter was that the Allies viewed de Gaulle as an unattractive personality; and whatever their supposed common interests, they did not get on. Even though Churchill recognised de Gaulle's importance early on, and announced that the Free French leader had a 'legal basis', it is clear that the two men never really saw eye to eye. On one level Churchill admired de Gaulle and what he was trying to do, and at times he was able to offer de Gaulle some financial support and general back-up. For most of the time though, he loathed the arrogance of de Gaulle and would often make life difficult for him (for example, by stopping his BBC radio broadcasts). The Free France leader recognised the problem:

> It must be said that the British authorities did little to help our efforts. Certainly they had distributed a leaflet advising members of the French forces that they could choose between repatriation, joining General de Gaulle and serving in His Majesty's forces. Certainly the instructions given by Churchill and the activities of Spears, whom the Prime Minister had made responsible for liaison between Free France and the British services, did sometimes succeed in vanquishing inertia or opposition. Certainly the Press, the wireless, many associations and countless individuals gave our enterprise a warm welcome. But the British High Command, which from one day to another expected the German offensive and perhaps invasion, was too much absorbed by its preparations to busy itself with a task which in its eyes was secondary.[104]

There was obviously a mutual fall-out. As Werth has written: 'Though financially dependent on them, de Gaulle continued to be arrogant and ungracious to the British.'[105]

The perspective of the US was very similar. Much to the chagrin of de Gaulle, the American government recognised the Vichy regime as the legitimate French authority. Roosevelt, in addition, seemed to think that de Gaulle was a potential dictator and irked him continually by calling his movement, 'the so-called Free French'.[106] If de Gaulle was put out by this, he was weakened almost fatally by the Americans' loyalty to Henri Giraud. After the liberation of Algiers in November 1942, the US was instrumental in planting a 'French authority' in Algiers which – deliberately – excluded de Gaulle. This was an amazingly explicit snub to de Gaulle, especially as Giraud was a neo-Pétainist (and thus symbolised the Americans' loyalty to Vichy, and not the Free French, as the 'legitimate France'). Eventually, after a lot of machinations, de Gaulle and Giraud became joint heads of the *Comité Français de Libération Nationale* (CLN) in Algiers. Ultimately, de Gaulle gained sole control of the 'provisional government' and the fallout was that, at the end of the war and later in the post-war period, he would have very little trust in the US and, furthermore, would make every effort to move France closer to the USSR in diplomatic terms. As Beevor and Cooper put it, de Gaulle's most pressing problem was not the internal resistance forces, but his relationship with the two Anglo-Saxon leaders.[107]

The Resistance also faced serious problems in its dealings with the colonies. Here the assumption was that the Empire was as much part of France as the mainland. Thus, de Gaulle set his stall out to win over all of France's colonies, but it wasn't easy for him to implement his plans. In September 1940, for example, in Dakar, West Africa, Vichy personnel forced the Free France forces to retreat – a serious setback for de Gaulle in his first efforts to swing Africa behind the Resistance. In Syria too, de Gaulle came up against problems. In Spring 1941 an Anglo-Free France force gained a military victory, but Britain – rather arrogantly in de Gaulle's opinion – tried to carve up the territory for herself. In the end Syria became French mandated territory under de Gaulle's provisional authority – a not entirely ideal outcome.[108] Elsewhere though, de Gaulle's efforts bore more fruit. On 27 October 1940 he became the legitimate guarantor of Brazzaville (*Conseil de Défense de l'Émpire*) and in the period that followed he established his own 'mini-empire' – taking in Chad, French Equatorial Africa and other parts of Central Africa.

Ironically – or perhaps predictably – the Liberation also brought problems, and 'insults', for de Gaulle. The fact of the matter was that Britain, the US and the USSR saw themselves as the key players in the Liberation. As such, they planned for an Allied Military Government of the Occupied Territories (AMGOT) to take power in post-war France and argued that 'American military governors' should be parachuted in to guarantee stability. In this sense, the Allies were ready to snub de Gaulle again. However, even though French forces played only a minor role in the 1944 Normandy landings (a marginal role that was, in effect, part of the Allies' plan), de Gaulle was eventually able to manoeuvre himself, and his own personal 'provisional government', into power amid the emotion and uncertainty of the summer months. As Werth states:

> De Gaulle was worried by the military role that the French themselves were to play in the liberation of their country – both as soldiers and as the Home Resistance; by the necessity of having France administered by Frenchmen, and not by AMGOT after the unfortunate model of Italy; and by the problem of how the Home Resistance, once it had outlived its usefulness, could be made to conform with the requirements of that central authority which he was determined to create.[109]

Thus, de Gaulle had plenty to concern himself with. Ultimately, the AMGOT authority was stillborn. To consolidate his position at the head of the newly-liberated nation, he devised a totally new republican infrastructure, which included commissioners of the republic, a consultative assembly, and a parliament body that would soon become a powerful symbol of post-war republicanism. Clearly, therefore, Shennan is correct to say that the Resistance and resistance activity stored up serious problems for the Liberation period.[110]

A movement of substance?

In evaluating the nature and essence of the French resistance, it must be acknowledged that there was never such a thing as 'the Resistance'.

Rather, what existed was an uneasy coalition of forces. Even though there was a common enemy – the German occupation force, with its accomplices at Vichy – each element in this 'alliance' had its own agenda and ideology.

Clearly, the Allies had a profound influence on events in 1944 and 1945, whatever de Gaulle said in later years. The Resistance in all its various forms had its triumphs and mini-triumphs, and definitely helped create a 'new spirit' in France,[111] but the reality of the situation was that for most of the time the Resistance was nothing more than a useful irritant. Throughout the Resistance, organisation and structure was poor; and whatever genuinely heroic activity did take place, the truth is that in 1944 the Allied war effort was the decisive factor.

It is also interesting that two historians – Cady and Shennan – have identified some common links between the Resistance and Vichy. Cady talks about the way that some vocabulary was shared and Shennan argues that, in their different ways, both the Resistance and Vichy stressed notions of authority and liberty.[112] This general point is well made and persuasive to a point. However, the similarities in language and rhetoric must not be exaggerated. It is not easy either to agree with those historians, like Andrews,[113] who have put forward the view that Resistance 'success' was nothing more than a 'myth'. Of course it is easy to criticise the overall effectiveness of the Resistance but it is another thing entirely to say that it was a minor player in the history of occupied France. Dreyfus says that in military terms the significance of the Resistance was marginal. However, he also makes the point that there were many different dimensions to the Resistance: the anti-Germanism of the early years, the political militancy of the communists and the emphasis on espionage and intelligence, to name but three.[114]

Ousby sums things up nicely: 'Though they might have been small in number, there were certainly *résistants* in France from the start, and so there was resistance, which grew from insignificance to play a part in how the drama of the Occupation was acted out.'[115] Kedward, however, should be given the last word:

> The events of 1942–4 put Pétain back into the fallible world of politics from which the process of mythification had elevated him. Historians with a weakness for cyclical theories of history like to suggest that the vacuum created was filled with a new myth, the

myth of the Resistance, and a new mythic figure, that of General de Gaulle. It is a tempting conclusion but a false one. Both Resistance history and Gaullism have been given an epic treatment which suggests a kind of myth-making, but no one who has seriously investigated the Resistance to Nazism, whether in France or elsewhere, finds it either easy or necessary to question its exceptional achievements. The history of Resistance may read excitingly as fiction. It reads even more effectively as fact.[116]

CHAPTER FOUR

Liberation

Freedom, hope and relief

Liberation was to be a new dawn: '*Ici commence . . .*'
Roderick Kedward[1]

'By 1944,' in the words of McMillan, 'it was certain that the Reich would not last a thousand years.'[2] As an event, the Liberation has elicited an array of verdicts and epithets. For Beevor and Cooper, it was all about 'love-making' and 'drinking'.[3] This may well be a romantic simplication, but it does convey the essence of the end-of-war occupation atmosphere: a mixture of jubilation, ecstasy and delirium. For Kedward and Wood, the Liberation was, rather, a profound and multifaceted phenomenon, with ramifications in all kinds of spheres: gender and overseas France to name but two.[4] McMillan argues simply that through the Liberation 'France was delivered from four years of bondage'.[5]

Whichever assessment one accepts, it is clear that this was an epoch-defining moment: like 1789, a landmark in French history whose significance and importance can be viewed in a whole range of different arenas. It is tempting to see the Liberation as an 'ending' – a fullstop that marks the termination of the wartime period. However, in a sense, the Liberation was much more than that, and should perhaps be viewed as a 'beginning'. (To keep the punctuation metaphor going: it could be seen as the start of a new sentence rather than the final stages of an old one.)

It is also very easy to fall into another trap: to believe that the Liberation was exclusively about joy, elation and untrammelled freedom, and to overlook the fact that, in reality, the years 1944, 1945 and 1946 were extremely difficult. Of course the Liberation period incorporated bliss and exultation, but it was also synonymous with violence and national division. It was a time, moreover, of wholesale recriminations; there was a constant fear of civil war and an ever-present awareness that France, if she was to survive in the post-war world, would have to put all her energy into national economic reconstruction. In this sense, the Liberation was a time of great trauma and tribulation, and not just unadulterated happiness and relief.

This chapter will narrate the main phases of the Liberation and then assess whether it was a specific event that can be linked to a time and place or whether it was more of an evolutionary process. It will also explore the interrelations, after 1944, between de Gaulle, the Free French, the forces of the internal resistance, the Allies and the ordinary French people. More specifically, the debate about who, or what combination of forces, actually achieved the Liberation will be considered. Was it de Gaulle who roused the nation into self-expression or was the contribution of the Allies the crucial ingredient in 1944? What role did the internal resistance play? We also need to be aware of two other debates: how was power transmitted in 1944, and in what kind of state did France emerge from the Liberation?

Beyond these issues, it will be interesting and necessary to explore the main themes that underpin the Liberation period. Hope, uncertainty, renaissance, unity, division, retribution, reconstruction were just some of these themes. What was their meaning and significance?

The process

It is commonplace to reduce the Liberation to one glorious and specific event.[6] Many onlookers take 26 August 1944 and de Gaulle's procession down the Champs d'Elysées as that one 'moment': the point in time – laced with symbolism – when freedom became a reality.[7]

It is natural, and to a certain extent predictable, that historians, and other onlookers, should desire – and actually locate – a defining moment for everything that the Liberation represented. And de Gaulle's famous Parisian stroll seems the ideal candidate. However, the Liberation of France was a complex process with a variety of intermediate phases and a series of significant dates:

8 November 1942	The Allies land in North Africa – the liberation of Algeria.
18 March 1943	Algeria is declared independent of the Vichy regime.
October 1943	The liberation of Corsica.
6 June 1944	The Allies land in Normandy.
25 August 1944	Paris is liberated.
September 1944	De Gaulle sets up the *Gouvernement Provisoire de la Républic Française* (GPRF) – the 'Government of National Unanimity'.
7 September 1944	Pétain and Laval are captured and taken to Sigmaringen in Germany.
15 September 1944	Special courts are organised for the *L'Épuration* (the purges).
23 October 1944	De Gaulle's GPRF is recognised by the Allies.
July/August 1945	The trial and sentence of Pétain.
January 1946	De Gaulle resigns as President of the GPRF after his draft constitution is rejected – he creates a 'non-party' *Rassemblement du Peuple Français* (RPF).
April/May 1946	Municipal elections are held.
October 1946	The Fourth Republic is established; Laval is tried and sentenced; legislative elections take place.[8]

It could be argued that the Liberation process straddled all the above events: from the 'mini-liberations' of 1942 and 1943 to the legal and constitutional developments of 1944 and 1946.

For Kedward the key to the issue is territory. He argues that the Liberation amounted to a series of small but significant advances:

The Liberation of France is first and foremost about territory, specific territory. It is about the fight for territory, and the reclaiming of territory. On 2 June 1944 this territory begins at Paulhac-en-Margeride. On 6 June 1944 it begins on the Normandy beaches; on 8 June, momentarily and tragically, it begins at Tulle in the Corrèze; on 15 August on the rugged coastline of Provence. It had already begun earlier, in November 1942 in Algeria, and in October 1943 in Corsica.[9]

'Mini-liberations' were happening all over France in the months pre-
ceding August 1944 (e.g. Corsica and Algeria)[10] and even after de
Gaulle's famous promenade in Paris there was still work to be done.
In this sense it is more accurate to think of the Liberation of a France
as a process, not as a moment. Kedward and Wood agree, arguing that
the Liberation was characterised, first and foremost, by 'diversity' and
'plurality'.[11] Ousby sums this view up neatly:

> Step by step, the occupiers were forced out of France in the last
> six months of 1944. There was no national date for liberation.
> Each town and village still celebrates a different date, the gaps
> between them marking advances that often looked bogged down,
> pockets of German defence that often turned out to be unexpect-
> edly tough.[12]

Whatever its exact parameters, the Liberation was a reality. Throughout 1944 the CNR had been planning for the moment. It demanded
political unity and economic reform. As it announced: 'A new Republic will be founded, which will sweep away the reactionary regime of
Vichy and return to our democratic and popular institutions the power
which they lost through the corrupting and treasonous activity that
preceded the surrender.'[13]

Transfer of power

The transfer of power at the Liberation was always going to be a deli-
cate process. As Larkin puts it: 'The Allied invasion of France con-
fronted both Vichy and de Gaulle with the problem of contriving a
transfer of power which would respect order and legitimacy yet would
leave the balance of moral dignity with oneself rather than with the
other side.'[14] Footitt and Simmonds are particularly interested in the
way that power 'on the ground' was claimed, and distributed, in 1944.
They paint a picture of a France that was hopelessly confused: myriad
local Liberation committees, significant regional variations, and a situation in which the Allies were gradually, and *willingly*, retreating – thus
leaving the field open to de Gaulle, the FFI, and other new organisations
and authorities. Though de Gaulle might present it otherwise, the tran-
sition of power was 'piecemeal' and far from seamless.[15]

Adjacent to this issue is the question of who was responsible for the Liberation. Kedward states in the introduction to *The Liberation of France*:

> Studies of the Liberation are complicated and sustained by the unending arguments about agency. These are due not only to rivalry between different strands within the Resistance narrative but also to the pivotal role of the allied *débarquements*. Tears welled up in the eyes of Pierre Boyer, a grain merchant in Saint-Affrique in the Aveyron, when he described the rows of American, British and Canadian graves in Normandy. He had been a *maquisard* at the liberation of Montpellier, but in 1991 he stated unequivocally that the French only participated in the national liberation. Ultimately, he said, they owed everything to the invading Allies. And what of the debts, less often recognised, to the troops from Algeria, Morocco, West and Equatorial Africa, and more distant French colonies, who fought in the liberating armies? The overwhelming case that France could only be liberated by invasion has never seriously been contested, and it is certainly not the intention of this book to do so, though the huge cost in French civilian lives, as well as Allied military lives, has to be confronted.[16]

The debate about agency is a complex one. It involves questions of political and military responsibility and, as Footitt and Simmonds make plain, it has always been affected by partisan concerns:

> By and large, Anglo-Saxon historians concentrate almost exclusively on the role of the Allies; their armies, their civil affairs officers, their political leaders and so on, with walk-on parts for the Free French and the Resistance . . . French historians on the other hand have devoted most of their attention to the role of the Resistance in the Liberation, giving little place to the Allies.[17]

This is an important point to note. More than most historical debates, the one surrounding the Liberation of France is cloaked in polemic, bias and myths. This is not surprising. So much was at stake in the Liberation, and so much depends on its legacy, that writers and rewriters of history have seized the opportunity to impose their own views.

Some writers have ascribed all to de Gaulle. The argument put forward is that de Gaulle ignited the flame of resistance; he was the key anti-Vichy and anti-German figurehead; he was the man who emerged to symbolise the reality of the Liberation in August 1944; and thus, when one is apportioning credit, de Gaulle must take his full share. The lack of modesty evident in de Gaulle's *War Memoirs* can also affect our judgement.

There is of course no doubt that de Gaulle was a central, if not indispensable, figure in both the Resistance and the Liberation. In Algeria he had created the CFLN and, as Jackson states: 'De Gaulle set about turning the CFLN into a government that could assume power in liberated France.'[18] By May 1944 the CFLN, under de Gaulle's tutelage, had metamorphosised into the GPRF. However, the exigencies of the situation de Gaulle found himself in, post-August 1944, led to him exaggerating his role in the Liberation.[19] In a sense it was natural for de Gaulle to overplay his involvement – he was by nature a vain and egotistical man – but in another sense it was a strategy. What de Gaulle found on his return to France in August 1944 was a nation ravaged economically and divided politically. If he wanted to inspire the country into reconstruction and revival – as he most certainly had to – he had to motivate the people of France into action and he had to make efforts to induce a feeling of hope. As Ousby says:

Men do not become leaders by popular acclamation just through shrewd political manoeuvring, though de Gaulle had certainly proved his mastery of this skill. Nor do they become leaders by popular acclamation just through the example of their courage, though de Gaulle had certainly set this example since June 1940. They become leaders by popular acclamation if they have a vision which answers a need, deeply and widely felt, and if they have at their command the language which makes people realise how deeply and widely they feel their need of the vision. De Gaulle had both the vision and the language. To a people who had spent four years humiliated and divided he had a healing myth to offer, a myth which promised to heal humiliation and heal division, which promised even to heal history. His rhetoric conjured the myth into life.[20]

One key strategy was to tell the population that both they and he had been intrinsic to the Liberation. This, in effect, was the art of myth-making. During the war – particularly early on – de Gaulle was reluctant to plan ahead, or even to talk about, the hoped-for future.[21] Perhaps this was a tactic; perhaps this was a rare piece of modesty.

Whatever the nature and extent of de Gaulle's involvement, the reality is that the people of France owed a profound debt of gratitude to the Allies – even if, at times, they may have been alarmed and put out by their arrogance. As Ousby states:

> Obviously it is not hard to challenge the Gaullist myth on its own, strictly historical, terms. France had not seen liberation by France, much less by the whole of France. She had been liberated by the Allied armies in which the French army formed only a minority, and by *résistants* who – though their numbers had grown as the Allied armies approached – were still, as they had always been, only a minority of the French . . . To offer even such a literal correction to the Gaullist myth is already to indicate the problems confronting de Gaulle.[22]

We know that the wartime relationship between de Gaulle and the Allied powers had never been cordial, and by 1944 it had deteriorated further. While de Gaulle saw the need to have one single French authority, the Americans had their own blueprint for France's future; at the same time they made it known that they would liaise with whatever French authorities they discovered *in situ*.[23]

In 1944 there was a point when Allied military leaders sought to minimise the involvement of de Gaulle and the indigenous French forces and to by-pass Paris in the military operation that ultimately brought liberation. Price argues that France's role in the Liberation was, all in all, 'limited'.[24]

It is also clear that tension between de Gaulle and the Allies carried over into the arena of practicalities:

> Roosevelt's intention was that liberated France should be administered by an American military administraton (AMGOT) and to this end American officials were receiving crash courses at Charlottesville in how to become French administrators; de Gaulle

meanwhile was preparing his own lists of 'Commissioners of the Republic' who would represent the GPRF in liberated France.[25]

This was not just a case of two different conceptions of the Liberation; this was a case of mutual hostility and antagonism. As McMillan has written: 'De Gaulle and the Free French abhorred the idea that not only might France be liberated solely by American and British troops but, even worse, the liberated *patrie* would be placed under an Allied Military Government of the Occupied Territories, as in the case of Sicily in 1943.'[26] De Gaulle's will may have eventually triumphed – AMGOT was 'stillborn'[27] – but the fact is that each 'side' was extremely unsure about the other's intentions.[28] This just added to the confusion and uncertainty.

We should also take account of the internal resistance and its role in 1944. Anarchic and unpredictable they may have been, but the France-based forces always believed that they would be a key part of the equation when the *dénouement* came. But, however much of a nuisance they caused, they could never escape the reality that both de Gaulle and the Allies looked down their noses at them. Kedward says that the FTPF, in particular, complained about the 'cautious' and 'submissive' role that others had delineated for them.[29] McMillan states:

> In planning the Liberation of Europe, the Allied strategists, in particular the Americans, had attached little importance to the contribution that internal resistance movements might make to freeing their own countries. Their role was to be confined to sabotaging German reinforcements and providing useful local intelligence. For leaders of the French Resistance such a role was deemed to be far from adequate to expunge the cruel memories of 1940.[30]

The debate about agency is long-running. As Kedward argues, '"Liberation by whom?" is not just a post-war controversy about the relative merits of Allied invasion, on the one hand, and arming the Maquis, on the other; it was an issue which occupied people's minds long before the summer of 1944.'[31] What was the role of de Gaulle? What was the role of the Allies? What was the role of the ordinary French people? These questions were being asked throughout 1944 and 1945; after the Liberation, the same questions were being asked. Perhaps the best strategy is Footitt and Simmonds'; they conclude that, 'there was not one Liberation of France but many.'[32]

In the aftermath of the Liberation a series of US posters tried to suggest that the Franco-American relationship was healthy and harmonious – and always had been. One announced: 'À LA FRANCE ÉTERNELLE SES AMIS, SES ALLIES'; another: 'LIBERTÉ, EGALITÉ, FRATERNITÉ . . . ENFIN.' A third was even more positive in its depiction of the relationship. It showed an American military policeman and a shapely French woman smiling massively as they travelled together by motorbike. The caption read: 'ENTENTE CORDIALE . . .!' These images idealised a diplomatic relationship which, in reality, was far from cordial.

Themes and cross-currents

If the process of the Liberation period is interesting and significant, the underlying themes are even more fascinating.[33] For, as much as at any other time in French history – if not more – there were fierce crosscurrents running beneath the surface of political life. They influenced all aspects of society and they affected the fears and aspirations of ordinary people. If one analyses the nature, tone and emphases of the new authorities' propaganda and publicity, one cannot help but be struck by the emphasis on certain themes and sentiments which add up to a significant statement about the nature of the French psyche c. 1944. Barber puts it nicely. He says that France and the French people were 'split between the impulse to explore the implications of calamity and to proceed as if nothing had gone wrong'.[34]

The most obvious theme was hope. After four years of darkness and hopelessness, there was, in the weeks and months following August 1944, a genuine sense of optimism. On the streets of French towns and cities there were celebrations and parties: a signal that hope had been restored. Price talks about the 'expectancy' in France and the desire for 'a new beginning'.[35] The feeling was that hope and enthusiasm had triumphed over apathy and resentment. It is in this sense that some historians have talked about the Liberation as a '*fête*' or a 'carnival'.[36]

Similarly, even though there was a fear of chaos and civil war, the belief was that somehow France *had to* survive. But twinned with hope was, perhaps, a more heartfelt sense of relief. After more than a thousand days of curfews and shortages, and Germans patrolling the streets, France once again was free. It is significant that de Gaulle entitles Volume 3 of his *War Memoirs* – the tome that dealt with the Liberation period – 'Salvation'. There was, most certainly, something spiritual and almost mystical about the Liberation experience.

The themes of hope and relief are very evident in official GPRF posters issued during 1944–45. In one, a woman standing on a special platform is lifting her arms to the skies; and behind her a large group of people are doing likewise. The look on her face suggests that she is happy, thankful, and hopeful. Another government-sponsored image is more ambiguous. It features a woman peering into the distance; she is looking into some kind of haze and is depicted raising her hand to her forehead. It is as if she is mopping her brow in relief – or shielding her eyes and her face from what she perhaps views as future problems for France.[37] Whatever their exact meaning, these two images are suggestive of the state of the French psyche in 1944 and 1945.

Hope and relief were central to the French mindset in 1944. We should not overlook the fact, however, that the nation was in a state of flux – not unnaturally, of course, given the turbulence of the wartime years. On many issues, there was serious uncertainty: How should post-Liberation France be governed? What was the best way to treat the wartime collaborators? How, and at what speed, should France rebuild?

For Kedward, the Liberation was an 'opening and a closure', a landmark period in which France 'looked backwards and forwards'.[38] It marked the end of German occupation and it saw the start of important social and economic developments. Women were rewarded for their wartime efforts with the vote. The communists advertised their yearning for some kind of 'national insurrection'.[39] More generally, the Liberation meant a start to economic reconstruction and what Price has called 'a massive social revolution'.[40]

There was also a growing feeling that France after 1944, in economic and political terms, was being born again. The key word was 'revolution'. Kedward dwells on this point:

> In his celebrated, but Delphic, message to the internal Resistance in June 1942, General de Gaulle claimed that '*le peuple français*' had condemned both the pre-War Republic and the Vichy regime, and he added, '*Tandis qu'il s'unit pour la victoire, il s'assemble*

pour une révolution.' Wresting the concept and promise of revolutionary change away from Vichy's '*Révolution nationale*' was one of the major recuperative aims of Resistance writing and action, inside and outside France. The term '*libération*' remained a stronger mobilising concept than the term '*révolution*', but the two shared many column inches in the clandestine press as if they were synonymous. Liberation was to be a new dawn: '*Ici commence . . .*'.[41]

There was not only a new political elite, but in time a new republican regime and a new set of parties and factions. Allusions to 1789 were common and revolutionary symbolism became fashionable once more. Kedward writes:

> The picture emerges of a period of euphoria when Resisters bridged the local vacuum of power with an assertive display of popular, patriotic ideals, setting up local committees to administer supplies, to organise recruitment for the army, and to relaunch their committees on a more equal, just and fraternal footing. There have been few occasions in French history since 1789 when the slogans of the Revolution have commanded such universal respect. For a month at least, before the weight of restructuring the economy and continuing the war began to sap people's optimism, there was a widespread belief that French society could be recast to give equal opportunities to everyone. It was an ideal to which resisters look back with pride. It was a period, say many, when very ordinary men and women were momentarily in charge of their own history.[42]

Revolutionary imagery is particularly evident in the celebratory posters published by the GPRF in August 1944. Two in particular are worthy of note. One, under the word 'LIBÉRATION', features a French-style Statue of Liberty; the inscription on the plinth reads 'LA FAYETTE'. Another features a Frenchwoman in classical revolutionary garb; the slogan swirling in the sky reads 'LIBERTÉ'.[43] The new French authorities were keen to assert that 1944 and 1789 were part of the same lineage: they both represented freedom and liberation.

The Liberation gave a strong impetus to artistic creativity. In the same way as the Occupation inspired writers and painters, so the Liberation, as a period and process, galvanised artists and intellectuals. As Barber writes:

> A burning moment of absolute anger and desolation in human history creates extraordinary impulses which remain with us and provoke, haunt and harass us. The Liberation of Paris in August 1944 and its aftermath is one such moment . . . It was a period of Europe's most intense and most creative self-exploration . . . After years of suppression and silence, liberated Paris was a vocal and visual eruption of cacophonic and panoramic dimensions.[44]

Barber goes further and talks about 'weapons of liberation'. In Paris, in 1944, he identifies 'weapons of art, weapons of performance and weapons of writing.'[45] Barber highlights the creative work of Genet, Giaconetti and Dubuffet in particular and argues that during the war France had not only suffered military invasion but, 'had been subjugated by language as well'.[46]

The purges

If there was something bright and healthy about the French attitude to liberation and revival, there was also something dark and sinister lurking within the French body politic. This, after all, was the era of the purges: an attempt to eradicate collaborators and collaborationists who had survived the war. From executions to beatings and head-shavings, *l'Épuration* was an exercise in vengeance. At times this campaign was organised and formal; at others anarchic and chaotic.[47] Ousby suggests there were two main phases of *l'Épuration*: 'rough justice' (1944) and 'the official creation of special courts' (mid-September 1944 onwards).[48] It would be accurate to look upon the *l'Épuration* as another element – albeit the most bloody – in *'la guerre franco-française'*, the spectre of which was to dominate and haunt France throughout the 1940s.[49]

It was perhaps inevitable that the sequel to war, occupation, collaboration and resistance would be blood-letting and a period of wholesale recriminations. The wartime era had been an emotional rollercoaster for France. After the Liberation France had to mete out a necessary amount of justice or, rather, had to be *seen* to be meting out a necessary amount of justice. As Ousby declares: 'Disaffected *résistants* on the one side and tainted *collabos* on the other, both required a firm hand. "Nothing can be done except through order", de Gaulle insisted.'[50] This was a tricky dilemma: punish too few collaborators and risk minimising the 'crime' of collaboration; punish too many and risk depicting France as a nation of collaborators – just when de Gaulle had a political interest in promoting the idea of unity and France as a 'nation of resisters'.

Even though Barber argues that 'Paris was a city obsessed with violence',[51] the general historical view is that *l'Épuration* was decidedly lenient. De Gaulle and the post-war authorities understood that they had to make an example of the most notorious collaborators – like Pétain and Laval – but in the end they shied away from a more comprehensive purge. They made great play of dealing with the most notorious offenders – but they left it at that.

So, in many ways the post-war purge was aimed only at identifying, and then punishing, a suitable – and smallish – number of people. Pétain and Laval were brought back to France for trial; they, along with people like Brasillach, were extremely useful high-profile scapegoats. As Beevor and Cooper argue: 'France knew that it could not face the post-war world until accounts had been settled with Marshal Pétain and Pierre Laval.'[52] In the end, and altogether, there were '100,000–150,000 deaths'[53] between 1942 and 1945. That said, the years of *l'Épuration* were extremely chaotic and anarchic, making it difficult to judge the scale of the post-war 'terror'.[54]

The purge was, by its very nature, calculated and cynical; because if every Frenchman 'guilty' of an act of collaboration was prosecuted half the population of the country would probably have been indicted. Retribution was harsh, but always pragmatic. The most apt conclusion must be this: in the immediate post-war period France exhibited an extremely strong desire for 'justice'; the process though was chaotic.

We also need to point out the relationship between *l'Épuration* and the intricate web of post-war myth-making. This link is best explained by McMillan:

Perhaps the most remarkable feature of the *épuration* was its relative moderation. Partly this was because de Gaulle was determined to prevent the outbreak of anarchy and civil war: violence had to be curtailed and minimised and the authority of the State upheld. Partly too, it was a question of preserving the myth of *la France résistante* in the interests of national unity. Hence, collaborators could be presented as a handful of guilty men (or women) unrepresentative of the nation as a whole.[55]

And as Ousby argues: 'In a sense the *épuration* continues today, or rather it has been resumed in the wake of Klaus Barbie's trial in the late 1980s.'[56]

If, in political and legal terms, the Liberation meant *l'Épuration*, in economic terms it meant reconstruction. This topic will be discussed at length in the next chapter – because in many ways it was an ongoing consequence or legacy of the wartime period. For the time being, it is important to note that during the Liberation period, as was the case in the decade or so following 1944–45, 'reconstruction' was the chief buzzword. A Ministry of Reconstruction was established and a state-sponsored 'propaganda' campaign proclaimed the intrinsic necessity of rebuilding.

Reflecting this, publicity posters, which only a couple of years earlier had been dominated by 'vulnerable' female figures representing 'invaded', 'occupied' and 'subservient' France, were now monopolised by strong men with bulging biceps: 'RETROUSSONS NOS MANCHES: ÇA IRA ENCORE MIEUX!', 'LES SOLDATS DONNENT LEUR SANG! LES METALLOS OFFRENT LEURS BRAS! TOUS AU TRAVAIL.'[57] In this new selection of posters, the economic challenge facing France in the Liberation years and beyond was likened, explicitly, to the military challenge that had faced the country between 1940 and 1944. Political and judicial adjustments had been made by the new liberation authorities; it was now time for the economy to take centre stage.

Unity and disunity

Dalloz argues that de Gaulle had two main aims in the weeks and months following his return to France: to re-establish state authority and to monitor the purges.[58] These were his twin priorities; the General believed that if he could accomplish both, the Liberation would proceed relatively smoothly. As it was, October 1944 emerged as a landmark date: De Gaulle's provisional government was recognised by the Allies. In the end though, there was something quite anticlimactic about this moment. Throughout the war, de Gaulle had been obsessed by the notion of 'legitimacy' – about what was, and was not, France's 'legitimate' government; ironically though, when it was achieved official recognition was 'something of a damp squib'.[59] Nevertheless, the Liberation was now complete: the occupiers had been removed, the task of moulding a 'new France' had begun, and a new political authority had been recognised. Kedward sums up the meaning of the Liberation. He says:

> For Vichy leaders, it was the moment when their subservience to Germany was fully exposed . . . For the internal Resistance, the Liberation was the triumphal justification of Republican patriotism, of anti-fascism and a faith in the fight for freedom which had seemed 'absurd' in 1940 . . . For the external Resistance, the Liberation was the moment when de Gaulle, the symbol of protest and resistance, became the embodiment of power.[60]

The Liberation was, as we have seen, a period of contrasts: hope – but at the same time uncertainty and relief; renaissance – but also retribution. The sharpest dichotomy was that between unity and division. On the one hand there was a huge and quite natural sense of unity during the Liberation and in post-Liberation France. The feeling was that the nation had emerged triumphant because of the toil of the French people and as a result of significant cross-class solidarity in the face of the occupier. The whole country, therefore, joined hands to celebrate its own success. After the war the notion of unity evolved into a very strong sense of partnership. Although there was much mutual suspicion evident in the relationship between the Gaullists and the communists in particular – the former feared a 'socialist revolution', the latter a 'de Gaulle dictatorship' – the exigencies of the situation encouraged the growth of tripartism: *Mouvement Républicain Populaire* (MRP) communist-socialist 'partnership'.[61] Whatever the tensions and frictions – and these were not insignificant – it was clear that Gaullists and communists-socialists had enough in common. This 'coming together' of traditional foes was a crucial and poignant aspect of the Liberation era.

Accompanying this feeling was an intriguing sense of continuity. It was impossible to ignore the profound dislocation that the wartime experience had brought. Despite this – or possibly because of it – de

Gaulle made a point of re-occupying his old War Ministry office when he arrived back in Paris; nothing, not even a world war, was going to alter his routine. It was also curious – and significant – that the people of France opted for a new constitutional arrangement (the Fourth Republic) that was almost identical in structure to the pre-war regime (the Third Republic). Bizarrely, 96 per cent of people voted against the continuation of the Third Republic in a special referendum . . . only to vote in favour of something extremely similar (the new 1946 constitution). Perhaps subconsciously, France did not really want to change, even after the shattering experience of world war.

For many historians, post-war 'unity' was just an illusion. According to this view, what existed in reality was a divided country, riven by bitterness and recriminations, and held together only by the cleverness and shrewdness of de Gaulle. In fact, his notion of 'a nation of resisters' evolved into a strategically useful myth. It implied that 'everyone' was a hero and 'everyone', therefore, could take the credit for the Liberation of France. In many ways, this was far-fetched – but it did help de Gaulle consolidate things in and around 1944 and it did, perhaps, prevent post-war France plunging into calamitous civil war. In time, onlookers were to become extremely cynical about this myth – they were to talk about bandwagon-jumpers, 'last-minute resisters' and the 'RMS' (*Résistance du Mois de Septembre*) – but in August 1944 a unifying myth, of whatever sort, was necessary.

CHAPTER FIVE

Legacy

An era still alive

> What surprised me most was not the passionate reactions – even
> among historians – to everything written about the 'dark years'
> of the war but the *immediacy* of the period, its astonishing pre-
> sentness, which at times rose to the level of obsession: witness the
> constant scandals, the endless invective and insult, the libel suits,
> and the many affairs that attracted the attention of all of France.
>
> Henri Rousso on 'The Vichy syndrome'[1]

It should come as no surprise to discover that the wartime period in
France – dramatic, traumatic and painful – has had a profound effect on France's national psyche in the post-Liberation period. We
should not suppose that the legacy has been simple and straightforward. Rather, we should regard the legacy as a complex and multi-
dimensional issue. It is a subject that continues to fascinate historians;
for example, Gildea entitles Chapter 3 of his history of post-war
France, 'Echoes of the Occupation'.[2]

The Liberation was the most immediate, and obvious, legacy of the
wartime period. The fact that the Liberation was not a specific event
in 1944, but an ongoing process, adds to this contention. France was
still being 'liberated' in 1945 and 1946 and, it could be argued,
beyond. But if we are to move away from the specifics of the Liberation, we find a whole range of legacies.

Beevor and Cooper identify three main issues in the immediate post-
war period. First, they highlight 'the settling of accounts' as a theme;
there was still bitterness and antagonism in the post-war period –
perhaps even more than there was during the Occupation. Second, they
point to France's sense of her own intellectual importance. As they

state: 'Almost immediately after the humiliation of the Occupation, and surrounded by the dilapidation and poverty of 1945, Paris rapidly managed to project its sense of cultural superiority.' Third, they highlight France's 'love–hate relationship with the United States'.[3] We will allude to all these themes in the course of this chapter.

It is also apt to cite the words of Maurois. He says that at the end of the war, 'the problems to be solved were vast'.[4] It is not surprising, therefore, that the legacy of the period was so all-embracing. Cottrell sums the situation up:

> It is impossible to overstate the confusion of feelings which Vichy, the war and the Occupation excite in France, even today. The simplified stories told by the small-town French war museums of evil German soldiers and heroic Resistance fighters are true enough. But so, too, are the more complicated stories of the complicities and collaborations of ordinary life, of Pétainism, of anti-Semitism, of the grey areas of wartime memory which can now be addressed to popular acclaim by films like *Uranus*, but which were for decades simply too painful for most people to touch.[5]

This last line is very poignant. Some specific aspects of the Occupation period remain 'too painful for most people to touch', but as we will discover, a new openness – of sorts – has emerged in recent years.

This chapter will be divided into two main sections. The first will explore the immediate legacy of the Occupation. The second section will take a broader view and assess the issue of legacy in the long term. It will become clear that in a whole range of spheres the wartime period is still very much alive.[6] Morris sums up the situation:

> Of all the various fashions which have preoccupied the French over the last two decades or so, perhaps the most evident and most sustained has been the all-embracing '*mode rétro*', that remarkable renewal of interest in, and extensive reevaluation of, the wartime occupation of France by Adolf Hitler's Germany.[7]

It should also be noted that many of the issues dealt with in the previous chapter are still relevant here. 'Liberation' and 'legacy' are, in a sense, related topic areas. Thus, we explored the significance of *l'Épuration* in Chapter 4, but we must acknowledge that the need for scapegoats was an ongoing one and continued into the post-war period. Similarly, we will deal with the subject of reconstruction in this chapter; but we need to be aware that the emphasis on post-war economic development was laid as soon as the war had finished and was a crucially important feature of the Liberation.

The immediate post-war years

Lottman might argue that the writers and intellectuals of the Left Bank enjoyed a post-war celebration that 'seemed to last for years',[8] but the reality of the situation for most ordinary people was confusion, uncertainty, division and 'disarray'.[9] Williams puts things into perspective:

> The war shook France out of the economic stagnation and political paralysis which had marked the last years of the Third Republic. Defeat provided the opportunity for a counter-revolution, directed not only against the working-class movement, but also against the democratic regime itself. The Resistance was a revolutionary response to this challenge, and its triumph produced an entirely new political situation. But the new-found national unity was quickly dissipated. The Communist drive for power forced all groups to take sides. During 1945 and 1946 there proceeded simultaneously a national effort at indispensable economic reconstruction, and a bitter 'cold war' between the ruling parties, which dominated the contemporaneous attempts to frame a new constitution. When the Communists went out of office in May 1947, the regime gradually returned to normal, and the political practices of the past slowly revived.[10]

The post-war period was never going to be easy, in economic or political terms. In particular, the need to 'cleanse' France after the horrors of collaboration was always liable to cause disruption – and this it did. There were widespread summary executions – in addition to the government-sanctioned ones – and, in places, a situation approaching anarchy. The fact that Laval and a small group of other key collaborators were executed in the immediate aftermath of the war is indicative of the attitude of the post-war regime. It is easy to exaggerate the extent of post-war dislocation. Cobban, for one, is aware of this; he claims that the speed with which France returned to normal and peaceful conditions after the war was far more impressive than is usually acknowledged.[11] This point should be borne in mind as we move on.

It is clear nevertheless that the competing claims of the various resistance groups helped to create a post-war climate which bordered on the frenzied. Everyone was manoeuvring for power and influence in the weeks and months following the Liberation – and not everyone was going to be satisfied. The Germans had been expelled from France but there was still significant tension between the communists' desire 'to impose a revolutionary view of the Liberation' and de Gaulle's powerful belief in the hegemony of 'established channels of law and order and state power'.[12] Gildea depicts this conflict as a battle between 'hardliners and soft-pedallers that was almost as important as that between those who won and those who lost by the act of Liberation.'[13]

This intra-resistance squabbling was not the only type of division – merely the most obvious. There was also the ever-present friction between ex-collaborators and ex-resisters and, less predictably, a serious divide among those who said they supported the new Fourth Republic. Cobban might argue that there were some elements of stability – like, for example, the *Quai d'Orsay* – but the overwhelming reality was that France was a society and a political entity torn into pieces.[14] It was de Gaulle who emerged as the leader of the nation, but in a precarious fashion. As Williams states: 'The rival government of General de Gaulle established itself at Algiers in 1943. It gradually obtained the recognition of the Allied powers, and took control in France in 1944. But until 21 October 1945 its authority was based on no formal or legal title.'[15] By 1946 de Gaulle's administration had been replaced.

It is difficult to underestimate the scale of the devastation suffered by France during the wartime years. A few statistics indicate the economic decline: a quarter of the nation's wealth was destroyed, industrial production in 1944 was only 38 per cent of the 1938 level; only half the nation's rail track survived the war, only a fifth of the country's lorries remained; in 1945 only two-thirds of French coal stocks were left, and half a million buildings were destroyed in the conflict.[16] In the aftermath of war, a 'Ministry of Reconstruction' was created, urbanisation quickened, and a population drift to the towns began.[17] It would cost France almost five million francs to return to normality.[18]

In time, long-range planning became *de rigeur*. The aim was '*une économie concertée*'[19] and France set out on the road to reconstruction with a ferocious appetite. The results were impressive:

GNP *(billions of US dollars)*
1948   16.3
1958   57.2

GNP *(per capita – US dollars)*
1948   387
1958   1,257[20]

France's post-war economic 'plan' was launched in January 1947, and in time Jean Monnet would add a European dimension to this national 'relaunch'.[21] Well into the post-war period, the constant preoccupation of France's political leaders was reconstruction. This could be seen in the policy emphases of the first post-war governments, in the language and rhetoric used by political leaders, and in the posters and propaganda advanced by the infant Fourth Republic. In time, the prioritisation of economic development and reconstruction by the post-war authorities had its own consequences: most significantly, an increased demand for immigrant labour.[22]

In the social sphere there were important developments – not least the granting of voting rights to women in 1946. However, as Collins Weitz argues, we should not assume that there was a definite 'cause' and 'effect' at play here. She insists that 'votes for women' was a pragmatic policy and not simply a 'reward'. She goes on to say that women's lives *were* changed and affected by the wartime experience, but not *just* by the award of suffrage rights.[23]

One of the most interesting, and understated, legacies of the Occupation period relates to foreign policy. Here we see two things happening. First, it is clear that de Gaulle's foreign policy position changed very little between the 1940s and the 1970s. The principles he adhered to at the start of the war were still conditioning his diplomatic attitude well into the post-war period. Jackson pinpoints two in particular: the belief that the nation state was a fundamental reality and, thus, that supra-nationality was a 'bad thing'; and the conviction that the independence of France was a prerequisite for national grandeur.[24] There were also similarities in the positions in which de Gaulle found himself: 'In 1958, as in 1944, de Gaulle's priority was to restore the activity of the state against the very forces which had helped him to power: in 1944 the Resistance, in 1958 the Algerian rebels.'[25]

In another sense, it is clear that the Occupation period conditioned the nature, and main thrust, of de Gaulle's post-war foreign policy. There was always a need to 'keep in the ranks of the Great Powers'.[26] However, de Gaulle's wartime experience – and his frosty relationship with Britain and the USA – made him believe that France should broaden her horizons as regards allies in the post-war period. Thus, even though organs like Le Monde made the case for a 'neutralist' foreign policy,[27] de Gaulle steered France towards the USSR and the Third World and away from Britain and the USA.[28]

In many ways this was a logical policy and in line with public opinion, for the 1940s and 1950s were years of severe strain in Franco-American relations. Clearly, de Gaulle's wartime disagreements with Roosevelt were an early sign of friction. In the immediate post-war years – even though France remained heavily dependent on the USA[29] – the relationship soured even more. In trade, culture and diplomacy there were conflicts and a general feeling of unease. As Kuisel puts it:

> Newsreels have captured for posterity the image of joyous crowds celebrating with GIs as Allied troops marched across the country in the summer of 1944. But liberation by outsiders only verified France's fall from grace. France had lost and America had gained in rank. This was the key political-psychological 'fact' of the early postwar era. Injured national pride, unacknowledged but real, filled the underground spring that fed anti-Americanism. A France already torn by internal division, humiliated by defeat, occupa-tion and collaboration, and slightly embarrassed by its liberation faced a crisis of national identity. The cultural revulsion against America, as one historian argues, may have been a kind of 'com-pensatory defence reflex' by which the liberated excommunicated the liberators.[30]

It should be noted that this in-bred anti-Americanism has lasted into the twenty-first century – particularly on the right and the far right.[31]

In the short term, however, the key legacy of the wartime period was another change of regime. The Third Republic had collapsed amid military defeat in June 1940; the Vichy administration had lost what limited power it did possess with the German invasion of the southern zone in 1942 (and imploded totally two years later); and in 1946 a series of constitutional arrangements were made to signify the establishment of the Fourth Republic.[32] The new republican regime was, ironically, extremely similar to the old one. Cobban claims that the 1946 constitution was 'closer to that of the Third Republic than the first draft had been ... The demise of the Third Republic may have been voted: its successor was to follow so closely in its steps that the observer might well feel that it had merely changed to remain the same thing.'[33]

In reality the new Republic did not do enough for enough people. De Gaulle felt it was too parliament-dominated, so he retreated, and went swiftly into exile.[34] The communists – even though they held power 'for nearly three years after liberation'[35] – felt that their goal of revolution was still a million miles away. Cobban estimates that the new Republic could rely on the support of barely half the nation.[36] It suffered because of this and within 14 years the Fifth Republic had been established. This demonstrated that France's perennial problems – constant political division and instability, and a profound inability to agree upon the 'right regime' – were still present, as they had been throughout the period 1789–1944.

Right and left

The confrontations and politicking of the Occupation period had significant consequences for the post-war era. Hewlett goes so far as to say that the political history of France 'continued to be particularly turbulent after the Second World War and the first 25 years after the war were in some ways more conflictual than the years 1900–39'.[37] His thesis is that whereas consensus politics prevailed in post-war Britain, Sweden and Germany, in France there was 'conflictual politics'.[38] Thus, right and left were still very much alive.

Whatever the qualifications and caveats – and many of course can be made – it is clear that de Gaulle and his associates emerged triumphant from the wartime years. As a consequence – and notwithstanding the odd setback – they came to dominate the politics of the three decades following liberation.[39] The Gaullist parties of the post-war period were to exploit the role of the General to the full and glorify him as saviour and liberator.[40]

For the extreme right – which must be clearly differentiated from the Gaullist right – the war and its aftermath meant temporary extinction. As Rémond has stated:

> In 1945 the hour finally seemed to have arrived when 'the End' could be written to the history of the Right. Everything was conspiring against it. Personnel suddenly was lacking. Its leaders were struck down: several were dead and others had let themselves be compromised with Vichy. All members of parliament who had voted full powers to Marshal Pétain on July 10, 1940 – and that included all of the Right Wing – were ousted from political life. Even those whose conduct had been irreproachable did not wholly escape suspicion and were required to justify their conduct, as if simply belonging to the Right was disreputable.[41]

Cheles *et al.* argue that the 'collapse of the Vichy regime drove the extreme right underground. In fact the right seemed to have vanished altogether.'[42] The post-war years brought doom and depression for the 'stigmatised' right and extreme right.[43] What credibility it had retained in 1940 was totally smashed by 1944. The execution of Laval and the imprisonment of Pétain were symbolic moments: the right had finally been castigated. As a result, in the years following the war – what Winock calls, 'two very gloomy decades'[44] – the right went into serious regression. Movements went undergound and political parties suffered at the hands of a vengeful and overtly anti-rightist electorate. Indeed, as Winock shows, the immediate post-war performance of the far right was pathetic – gaining only 1.5 per cent of the popular vote in the Legislative elections of June 1951.[45]

It is Milza, however, who notes that by 1960 'neo-fascism' was benefiting from the conjunction of three favourable factors: 'the survival, during the vicissitudes of the immediate post-war, of collaborationist fascism, the acceleration in the pace of economic change, and lost colonial wars'.[46] Indeed, all these factors played a part. However, it was with the Algerian War of 1954–62 – and the new traumas that this inflicted on France – that the right gained its first significant opportunity to regroup and reform. This was done spectacularly through the *Algérie Française* movement. This political grouping was dominated by hardcore nationalists who demonstrated a powerful, die-hard belief in the 'Frenchness' of Algeria and opposed all moves designed to give Algeria more independence – especially those initiated after 1958 by the new President, de Gaulle. On the mainland it was a movement of extremists and fascists – including Jean-Marie Le Pen – while in North Africa it was dominated by army personnel and French settlers (*pieds noirs*). The pro-*Algérie Française* attitude was fuelled by 'memories of de Gaulle's refusal to grant a pardon to the geriatric Marshal Pétain (who died in gaol in 1951), and was prompted by his "betrayal of the army's trust" in having negototiated with the FLN'.[47] Sores still ran deep and de Gaulle – in the eyes of some – was now connected with *two* shameful episodes in twentieth-century French history. The right, though, was back in business. Winock uses the phrase '*des clandestins aux activistes*' to describe this re-emergence.[48]

The Poujadist outburst of the late-1950s was also, in some ways, a legacy of the wartime period. Pierre Poujade, a small-town stationer established a movement to speak for, and to look after the interests of, French shopkeepers. The movement gained 53 seats in the 1956 legislative elections and frightened many people into thinking that Poujade – a man likened in the national press to Hitler – could topple the Republic. In the end this never happened, and in retrospect was never likely to happen. For us, though, the significance of Poujadism lies in its origins. In that Poujade's *Union de Défense des Commerçants et Artisans* (UDCA) movement included a number of ex-Vichyites eager to return to political action, it could be viewed as a key moment in the history of post-war France.[49] More importantly perhaps, Pou-jadism can be interpreted as a *cri de coeur* on behalf of all those people affected in an adverse way by post-war reconstruction and moderni-sation. Poujadism was thus a notable, if indirect, legacy of the wartime years. The fact that the UDCA and the *Algérie Française* movement were born almost simultaneously suggests that after a short and painful interval – when it was licking its wounds – the right was back. This was a big surprise. Rémond says that in the immediate post-war years:

> Many did not hesitate to announce the definitive end of the right as a political force and even as an ideology. Ten years later it was possible for Marcel Merle to write, 'Weighing everything carefully,

perhaps the most important political phenomenon of the regime's (Fourth Republic's) history was this reconstitution of a Right that everyone, hopefully, or scornfully, had agreed to condemn.'[50]

In time – and as a result of wholesale amnesties[51] – former Vichy loyalists came to dominate the movements, parties and groups on the post-war right. *Algérie Française*, Poujadism, *Jeune Nation* and, much later, the *Front National* all provided a home for ex-Vichyites and ex-collaborators.[52] In time too, the ideas of Vichy were to resurface in the programme and ideology of some of these groupings. In 1969 Rémond summed up the legacy of the Pétain regime:

> The importance of the Vichy episode in the history of the Right Wing demonstrates that the historic significance of events is not necessarily proportionate to their duration. Although the Vichy regime lasted only four years and the Liberation caused the disappearance of both its personnel and its institutions, the National Revolution nevertheless had important consequences for the destinies of the Right. It revealed the permanence of aspirations and ways of thinking that were believed outworn by the longevity of the Third Republic; it incarnated a hope of the Right. It left memories and regrets which even today are not completely dead: currently one faction of the extreme Right Wing can be distinguished by its loyalty to the government of Marshal Pétain and its unquenchable faith in the legitimacy of the French State as the basis for its anti-Gaullism. Above all, the public's identification of the Right with the unhappy Vichy experiment discredited this faction for a long time. It dealt a blow that may be fatal to one form of extreme Right Wing nationalism.[53]

This interim verdict was perhaps premature. The rise and consolidation of the *Front National* as a well supported political party in the 1980s and 1990s proved that the ideas of the nationalist right still had a constituency.

Whereas the right suffered post-war, the left blossomed. Indeed, the new parties of the left were to become instrumental in the shaping of the new France. Not only this but the main political groupings on the left have invariably looked back on the period of the Resistance as a formative one, as one of heroic action and brilliant symbolism. Today's

Communist Party in particular has made great play of its role in the Resistance. This may be justified, but one cannot help feeling that its declining popularity in the 1980s and 1990s made nostalgia for the Occupation period a pragmatic necessity.

Most potently perhaps, there is Pétain's legacy. In the decades following the Liberation, he was to provoke both hatred and idolatry. It started with his trial and his imprisonment, and burgeoned from there. Griffiths explains the origins of the Pétain cult:

> Pétain was not a criminal. He was a man who, through vanity and a misunderstanding of events, had led his country into the wrong paths ... On 15 August he was condemned to death; though on account of his great age, the Court asked that the verdict should not be executed. For the next six years, until his death on 23 July 1951, he was kept in prison on the Île d'Yeu, deteriorating both mentally and physically. The inhumanity of the imprisonment of this old and senile man, from the age of 89 to 95, will go down in history as one of the examples of the barbarity of our age. It has also served to add to the pious hagiology which now, for many, surrounds the figure of the Marshal.[54]

In the post-war years, Pétain's credibility as a patriotic national figure would decline sharply; but his memory would be powerful enough to provoke hardline followers into establishing special pro-Pétain movements and organisations. Anderson mentions the significance of the *Association pour Défendre la Mémoire du Maréchal Pétain*.[55] He says that it was difficult for most ex-Vichyites to regain power and influence in the late-1940s and 1950s, so most settled for unadulterated nostalgia: one key demand was for the body of the Marshal to be transferred to Douaumont 'to lie among those who had fallen at Verdun in 1917'.[56]

Whatever the fortunes of left and right, we should not forget that the immediate post-war era was also a period of *tripartisme*.[57] This phenomenon – the rule of the three main parties (the MRP, the PCF and the *Section Française de l'Internationale Ouvrière* [SFIO]) in coalition – was a unique development. The philosophy that lay behind it could be traced back to the war, its immediate aftermath and the general feeling that France and its politicians should act in a more mature, sensible and consensual manner. Although the experiment of *tripartisme* lasted only until 1947, it should be viewed as an important legacy of the wartime period.

Myth against myth

In the long term, the legacy of Vichy has been just as powerful as that of the Resistance. It has been an era – and an *issue* – that France, as a nation, has struggled to cope with. More than that, it has become a taboo subject that very few people have wanted to discuss.

For three decades or more, Vichy was a topic that ordinary people did not talk about in respectable company. Even less did governments make statements about it. This was partly through guilt (the country was ashamed) and partly through common sense (the leaders of post-war France had a significant interest in fostering 'unity', however artificial). De Gaulle made strenuous efforts to bolster the view that wartime France was a nation of resisters and that France, alone, had been responsible for her own liberation:

> Paris! Paris humiliated! Paris broken! Paris martyrised! But Paris liberated! Liberated by itself, by its own people with the help of the armies of France, with the support and aid of France as a whole, of fighting France, of the only France, of the true France, of eternal France.[58]

As Rousso implies, de Gaulle at this point was fantasising about France's role in the Liberation. He was exaggerating the role of Paris and France, underplaying the contribution of the Allies, and papering over the cracks of post-war division and disunity. Judt claims that 'it suited almost everyone to believe that all but a tiny minority of the French people were in the Resistance or sympathised with it. Communists, Gaullists, and Vichyists alike had an interest in forwarding this claim.'[59] It was de Gaulle though who had most to gain from introducing this 'resistancialist myth'.[60]

De Gaulle's task, however, was a tricky one. He wanted to emphasise the idea that France liberated herself, but he did not want to glorify any one resistance organisation lest he entangle himself in intra-resistance disputes or appear too overtly as wanting to rewrite history.[61] Thus, as Rousso points out, the myth that emerged celebrated 'a people *in resistance*, a people symbolised exclusively by the "man of June Eighteenth" [de Gaulle], without intermediaries such as political parties, movements or clandestine leaders'.[62] Judt agrees with this general line of analysis:

> The initial postwar myth claimed that although the fighting Resistance may have been a minority, it was supported and assisted by 'the mass of the nation', united in its desire for a German defeat . . . In order to put Vichy behind . . . postwar France resorted to a strange self-induced amnesia, strange in that it took place in broad daylight, so to speak, and in the face of common knowledge of the truth. At one and the same time, France undertook to purge itself of the most obvious collaborators, while putting behind it the memory of the indifference or ambivalence of the majority.[63]

In all of this France seemed to be deluding herself. McMillan helps to put things in perspective. He estimates the number of resistance activists and concludes: 'At best . . . only a maximum of 2 per cent of the French adult population can be deemed to have been "in the Resistance" – a figure strikingly at odds with the myth of *la France résistante* developed at the Liberation.'[64]

Already, therefore, we see doubt being cast on the notion of France as a 'nation of resisters'. This is no real surprise, for it was, first and foremost, a tactic or strategy – a point that de Gaulle came close to acknowledging on occasions. Larkin tends to concur: 'For the nation's own morale, and in order to present a united French front to other countries, the internal split between the former supporters of Vichy and the Resistance had to be healed.'[65] The same point is made by McMillan:

> The Resistance was important as an enormous boost to French morale . . . In permitting Frenchmen to have some share not only in their own liberation but in setting the whole of Europe free from the Nazi yoke, it gave back to a great nation its sense of dignity and pride.[66]

So, in many different ways the Resistance 'myth' served several useful purposes: it bound a nation together, it helped de Gaulle politically, and it made French people – *all* French people – feel good about themselves (at least for a short period). And whether we call it 'the Gaullist resistancialist myth', 'the myth of *la France résistante*', or merely 'the Resistance myth', we are talking about the same useful construct.

The decades after 1945, however, witnessed a number of developments that jeopardised the continued existence of the myth. Rousso argues that the revolution of 1968 made many people view the past in a different light and the accession of Pompidou to the presidency brought to power a man with an open scepticism about the nature and reality of the French Resistance.[67] However, it was the release of the film, *The Sorrow and the Pity*, that was to be the most explosive event. As Webster has written: 'Marcel (Ophuls) took personal revenge on Vichy with a 1971 film ... revealing the extent of anti-semitism in Vichy's chief satellite town, Clermont-Ferrand.'[68] This documentary, which was particularly vivid and honest in its analysis, gave a lie to the myth which had grown up since 1944 and which said that France was 'a nation of resisters'. The film's strategy was to 'out' collaborators and to leave ordinary French people – those who had been born after the war – in no doubt as to the reality of the politics, and political choices, in wartime France. The appearance of Rousso's book, *The Vichy Syndrome*, in 1987 also made people reflect: if France was so 'innocent' – as the Gaullist myth inferred – why did nobody really want to discuss, or even acknowledge, the Vichy years?

The Mitterrand era

The dawn of the Mitterrand presidency in 1981 gave free rein to new 'revisionist' attitudes. The socialist president began to make keynote pronouncements on the Vichy period and, more significantly, the authorities made tentative plans for a round-up of suspected 'war criminals'. Over a decade or so – a period that spanned the 1980s and the 1990s – three of the most famous French collaborators were put on trial: René Bousquet, Paul Touvier and, most recently, Maurice Papon. This created a quite distinct climate in France. One commentator has talked about 'the renewed desire to punish people for war crimes 45 years after the end of the war';[69] another has spoken of 'the purge today'.[70]

The Bousquet affair began in 1949 when he was sentenced to a three-year jail term for his actions during the war. It was in 1978, however, that the full extent of his wartime record was discovered. A decision to try him again, on charges of 'crimes against humanity', was made in 1990. The *Daily Telegraph* commented on France's new openness:

> Something has gone wrong in the French mechanism for ensuring that some of the very dirty laundry left over from the Nazi occupation does not get a public washing. Against strong official urgings, a Paris court decided last week that the case of the former Vichy police chief René Bousquet should not be sent up a legal blind alley.[71]

This passage hints at something quite profound: a fresh determination to unearth as much of the Vichy story as possible, whatever the consequences or ramifications. Most onlookers would view this as a positive development. The Bousquet saga was symptomatic of something far bigger. In 1942 Bousquet had been appointed Minister of the Interior in the Vichy government. The accusations against him involved not just one man, but a whole system of government. As Cottrell wrote at the height of the controversy: 'Bousquet represents . . . the last chance to put the Vichy regime on trial for the worst of its crimes.'[72]

It is clear from the headlines that accompanied the Bousquet case that a regime was being judged: 'A FIGHT TO PUT WARTIME NIGHTMARES TO REST', 'WAR CRIMES TRIAL OPENS OLD WOUNDS', ANXIOUS TIMES FOR THOSE WITH DIRTY WAR LAUNDRY' and 'JUDGEMENT ON VICHY'.[73] However, although the country was strongly determined to come to terms with its wartime 'demons', there is also some evidence to suggest that it did not want the exposure to go too far. Cottrell, for instance, has argued that the French establishment was initially very keen to keep the Bousquet case away from the courts.[74] Similarly, it is claimed that the Elysée was not pleased to learn that the Bousquet case was to be reopened.[75] That said, the indications are that Mitterrand displayed both an enlightened attitude and a new openness towards the concept of war trials in the 1980s and the early 1990s.

The case of Paul Touvier was not dissimilar to that of Bousquet. The *Independent* reported in May 1989:

> After 45 years on the run, Paul Touvier, a French war criminal, has been tracked down and arrested in a traditionalist Catholic

priory in the centre of Nice. His arrest brings to an end one of the longest manhunts in French history. Touvier headed the militia which helped Nazi occupation forces track down resistance fighters. Police believe he worked closely with the Gestapo chief, Klaus Barbie, who was jailed for life in France in 1987 for war crimes.[76]

The fact that Touvier was arrested for 'crimes against humanity' was the main aspect of the story. For us, however, the Touvier case reveals other significant things about the legacy of the Vichy period. First, it is clear that some individuals in modern-day France do not support an anti-Vichy 'witch-hunt'. For example, *Front National* leader Jean-Marie Le Pen responded to the capture of Touvier by saying: 'The police must have plenty of time on their hands if they can hunt down such a feeble old man.'[77] Le Pen is one person who would like to lay Vichy's ghost to rest, perhaps for personal reasons.

For Patrick Marnham the key aspect of the situation was that Touvier could not hope to receive a fair trial. He refers to the 'doubts as to whether it was possible to try a man for crimes in which most witnesses and victims were long since dead. It also raised the possibility that the charges against Mr Touvier had been brought out of loathing for the deeds he is accused of rather than out of any satisfactory evidence.'[78] Here again we see the legacy of the wartime period in all its vividness; there has been so much polemic that it is hard to separate the fantasy from the fact.

In the aftermath of Touvier's arrest, a national opinion poll revealed that 37 per cent of French people thought it 'normal' that a religious order should have protected him.[79] Was this a statement about the role of the Catholic Church in contemporary France? Did the poll finding indicate that a significant minority of the French population wanted Touvier to escape the police? Did people want to see an end to the escalating legacy of the war? Whatever the exact significance of the survey, it is clear that the Touvier case was still provoking controversy.

These cases are interesting, but we should not lose sight of their real importance. They show how the legacy of the wartime years lives on; the extent to which France has had to consider the question of what is, and is not, a 'war crime' or a 'crime against humanity';[80] and, also, how acutely aware of its responsibility to dispense real justice the French nation now is. President Georges Pompidou, who officially pardoned Touvier for his wartime activity, attempted to put the issue into perspective:

> For more than 30 years our country has suffered one national crisis after another. There was the 1939 War and the humiliations of defeat; the horrors of the Occupation, and the excesses of the purge which followed the Liberation. Then there was the war in Indo-China and the terrible conflict in Algeria which led to the forcible displacement of a million Frenchmen who were chased out of their homes ... I myself was denounced to the Gestapo by the Vichy government and have since survived two assassination attempts. So I think I have the right to ask, are we going to keep our national wounds bleeding for ever? Hasn't the time come to let the curtain fall and forget those days when the French loved each other so little that they tried to kill each other?[81]

Pompidou made this comment in 1971. Since then a new millennium has dawned, but the question he raised has still to be resolved.

Klaus Barbie, a German agent based in France, and Maurice Papon were also put through the same imperfect process as Bousquet and Touvier.[82] On the whole, France's 'war trials' have been followed eagerly by the media and the general public alike. They have also been instrumental in restoring – if only in part – France's integrity and credibility with regard to accepting, and acknowledging, her wartime experience.

We should, however, strike a note of caution here. As Webster writes:

> Although public interest in Vichy's complicity in the murder of thousands of Jews has increased since the trial of Klaus Barbie in 1987, there is still a large measure of indifference shown by local and central governments. Most concentration camp sites have disappeared altogether and where there are commemorative signs the emphasis is always on Nazi cruelty with no mention of French complicity. The official protection as a classified monument given to the German concentration camp and gas chamber at Natzweiler-Struthof can be compared to the neglect at one of the most notorious Free Zone camps at Gurs in the Pyrenees.[83]

The irony of the whole situation was that Mitterrand – the man who had done so much to open up the Vichy era to scrutiny – was accused of having skeletons in his own cupboard. The whispers about Mitterrand's past had emerged intermittently during his presidency (1981–95), but reached fever-pitch in 1994, on the publication of Pierre Péan's book on Mitterrand's early political development, and in January 1996, after his death.[84] The veteran socialist politician was accused of many things: working for Vichy, receiving its patronage, honouring Pétain, aiding officials of the wartime government who attempted to avoid arrest, and maintaining a longstanding friendship with Bousquet.[85] As Friend has argued: 'Mitterrand carefully retouched the history of his early youth in the Vichy period.'[86] Commentators were extremely dubious about Mitterrand's activities when they came to weigh up his life:

> Not until the last years of François Mitterrand's life did the spectre of Vichy and his hitherto obscured role in the French collaborationist government cast a long dark shadow over his career . . . The row that erupted over his Vichy past may have surprised M Mitterrand. He did not believe in moral absolutes and insisted life was never a question of black and white but, in his own words, 'light grey and dark grey'. If that were so, M Mitterrand's Vichy years were still among the darkest shades of grey.[87]

> After the Third Republic's fiasco, the Pétainist interlude and the shambles of the Fourth Republic, the absence of self-confidence was Mitterrand's opportunity. Evidently here was a broker and a juggler by instinct, a man who could find his way through, and satisfy all parties by identifying with none exclusively. It was more than a symbol that he used to pay pilgrimages to the grave of the disgraced Pétain and that he maintained his friendship with exploded collaborators of the stamp of René Bousquet, the Paris chief of police who signed the accord placing the *gendarmerie* at the orders of the Nazis.[88]

> What was remarkable was that the ageing Mitterrand seemed completely at ease with friends he had made in the 1930s and remained unflinchingly loyal to them. The President admitted quite happily

to one of his biographers, Pierre Péan, that his circle included members of the Vichy-era interior ministry responsible for rounding up and deporting thousands of Jews . . . As President he never officially apologised for the crimes of Vichy, and . . . continued to send a wreath to the tomb of Marshal Pétain on the Île d'Yeu.[89]

It is not surprising, therefore, that Cole sums up Mitterrand's wartime record in the three words, 'courage', 'captivity' and 'ambiguity', and Laughland describes the former president's relationship with Vichy as 'intriguing'.[90]

The legacy of the Occupation period is a profound one. Even though, in time, Mitterrand joined the Resistance and moved to the left,[91] his association with the Vichy regime has been stigmatised by onlookers – as if identification with the administration, in itself, equates to some kind of horrible crime. That, to be sure, is the power of the wartime period.

France today

The war years have left their imprint on modern-day France. It is pertinent to analyse the manner in which France has coped, or failed to cope, with the memory of collaboration and resistance and full-scale civil war. Burrin has written:

> The years of occupation indubitably left a painful splinter lodged in the memories of French people; for a cherished image of France was damaged by all the compromising deals struck with one of the worst regimes of modern Europe. The experience of the Second World War overturned the glorious image of the Great War, which had not only ended in victory, but had also produced a sacred unity in times of tribulation.[92]

And we should not be deceived: the wartime period is still an issue at the beginning of the third millennium.

For a start there is a political party, the *Front National*, which is still acutely aware of the Occupation years. In its rhetoric and discourse, the FN continually makes both overt and covert references to the wartime period. In recent years it has talked about an immigrant 'invasion' and 'occupation'; it has labelled those in power *'les collabos de décadence'*; and it has talked about the need for all FN members and supporters to 'resist' heightened immigration levels and governmental policies that, in its view, put the best interests of France in jeopardy. Likewise, in the pages of the FN's journals and mainstream newspapers, the wartime period is still a subject for debate. Occupation-related topics are still big news – in particular the issue of the treatment of Jews. The FN has advanced a rather unpleasant form of anti-semitism: making jokes, playing on words, and generally trivialising the experience of Jews during the Second World War and in France today. Fenby argues that the rise of the FN, together with other social and political developments, poses an acute problem for modern-day France: 'Forty years after Charles de Gaulle gave it a new lease of life, France is again a nation at risk.'[93]

These references to the most sensitive aspects of the Occupation in FN discourse are not just haphazard. Rather, they are part of an extremely well thought out strategy that likens the current immigrant 'threat' to the Nazi danger in the early-1940s. It is difficult to deduce the success of such a tactic, but its significance is clear: the wartime period is still very much alive. Webster is particularly interested in the anti-semitic issue:

> The spirit of Vichy's unrepentant anti-Semites is still alive, nur-tured by politicians like the National Front leader, Jean-Marie Le Pen, who has twice been charged with making anti-Semitic remarks and by the anonymous Jew-haters who dug up the body of an eighty-year-old man in the Jewish cemetery at Carpentras in 1990 and tried to impale the corpse. Perhaps it was the nation-wide protest against this sign of resurgent anti-Semitism that per-suaded the Paris city council to end a long controversy and allow Léon Blum a little posthumous revenge.[94]

It would also be true to say that modern-day France is getting better at remembering, commemorating and, in general, being far more open about wartime events. On this matter Webster mentions a recently established memorial to one of Barbie's most gruesome war crimes and a new outpouring of information about the Drancy concentration camp in Paris.[95] On a more positive note, it has been recognised that Vichy's emphasis on planning and technology and many of its agricultural reforms had a constructive impact in the decades following the Liberation.[96]

Historians of France are often reminded of the ever-present legacy of the French revolution. A student once asked his teacher: 'When did the French Revolution end?' The teacher replied: 'We're still waiting'. A similar kind of point could be made about the Occupation and its legacy. As Kedward and Wood state:

> It could well be argued that the identity of contemporary France is rooted in the history of Vichy and the Resistance in the same way that nineteenth century France was rooted in the Revolution of 1789. If that seems too bold a claim it must at least be granted that French republicanism today could not be defined without detailed reference to the Resistance, and that controversy about Vichy and collaboration has grown and not diminished with time. In both respects the Liberation of France is a pivotal image and event.[97]

There is, as we have seen, a never-ending fascination with the war, the reality of the Nazi invasion, and the issues and controversies at play during and immediately after the conflict. Perhaps in this new century, with generations replacing generations, the legacy of the Occupation may diminish. Or maybe it will not.

Evaluation

Issues and themes

At the beginning of the twenty-first century, the subject of the Occupation still provokes historians and unnerves ordinary French people. In one sense the wartime period is just a dusty historical era; in another, it is radically different. It is different because the period has the power to perplex and haunt. It is very easy to say that an historical period is still 'alive' half a century and more afterwards, but if ever an era deserved and warranted such an epithet, it is this one.

In Chapters 1, 2, 3 and 4 we explored the Occupation, the Vichy regime and collaboration, the Resistance and the Liberation as if they were routine historical topics. This of course is not the case. 'Occupation' is a term with striking overtones, even 60 years on. The Occupation of 1940–44 was not the first time that France had experienced – and suffered – foreign invasion and subjugation. As such, the modern-day French national psyche is extremely sensitive to the notion – *any* notion – of foreign occupation. This is reflected in, for example, Le Pen's constant depiction of the contemporary immigrant influx as an 'invasion' and 'occupation'. The FN leader knows that this language will strike a chord with ordinary French people.

Likewise, the term 'Vichy' still has a particularly powerful resonance in contemporary political debate: it can stir up all kinds of horrible memories for people, it can signify political betrayal and dishonesty, and it can conjure up images of a weak, humiliated and fallen nation. The town of Vichy is still fighting hard to rid itself of an unpleasant stigma.

The word 'resistance' also has a mesmeric effect – but in a positive, and not a negative, way. Even though, as we have discovered, the Resistance 'myth' – devised and peddled by de Gaulle – has been demolished, the phenomenon of anti-German, anti-Vichy political activity still excites people. Today, not only are memories of the Resistance represented in veterans' associations and in an array of potent commemorations and anniversaries, but in general terms there is an undimmed magic associated with the word.

It may be argued that France is still in *the midst of* liberation. The feeling exists that France, six decades on, is still confronting and still dealing with her demons. There is still introspection and embarrassment where the war years are concerned, and still a tendency to wallow in self-pity and shame. Today, amid war trials and wartime revelations, and with coy references to the occupied period still fashionable, the Liberation does not appear to have come to a final close. France may now be at the heart of the European Union – in tandem with the 'new' Germany – but in reality the wartime period still conditions the mindset of twenty-first century France.

Several key points and themes need highlighting. First, if the wartime years meant anything they meant division. Most obviously, there was division and friction between resisters and collaborators – a fundamental divergence in outlook. This confrontation evolved into civil war and what some commentators call '*la guerre franco-française*': a confrontation between those who believed in liberation and an independent, unoccupied France and those whose vision of the future was dominated by the notion of a new Hitler-dominated Europe. Other divisions also emerged: between rich and poor and between haves and have nots; between peasants and town-dwellers and between southerners and northerners; between the working class and the upper class and between younger generations and older generations. So the German-constructed demarcation line split France in two – not just in geographical terms, but in social, economic and political terms as well. These divisions served to create a nation disabled by friction.

Second, life in occupied France was about choices. For individuals, families and organisations, there were crucial and life-affecting choices to be made constantly. To remain in the occupied zone – or not? To join the exodus to the free zone – or not? To resist – or not? To collaborate – or not? These were profound moral and ethical dilemmas. Not for nothing, therefore, is Sweets' study of France under the Occupation entitled *Choices in Vichy France*.[1] The fact of the matter was that throughout the Occupation, French people had decisions to make

– fundamental decisions that would affect the essence of their lives and livelihoods.

Third, was the Occupation period an end or a beginning? The simple answer is that it was both. The Fall of France marked the death of the Third Republic and the birth of the new (but also old) Pétain regime and the ultra-traditionalist project that was the National Revolution. In time, the Occupation years would witness the collapse and eclipse of Vichy, the Liberation, and the dawn of a new era in the form of de Gaulle's provisional government and the Fourth Republic. In this respect, therefore, the wartime period was a watershed: an end, but also a beginning.

With hindsight it is now no longer satisfactory to depict the Occupation as merely a confrontation between 'the good' (the resisters) and 'the bad' (the Germans and the collaborators). What this study of occupied France has shown is that there were many varieties of response. 'Passive collaboration' and 'passive resistance', for instance: these are complex matters that defy easy categorisation and go to prove that the wartime era was a period in which individual Frenchmen and women were forced to make crucial and life-affecting choices. If there was something heroic and idealistic about resistance and the decision to resist, there was something dark and sinister – and perhaps also understandable – about collaboration and the decision to collaborate.

The men who personified these two stark options were once colleagues and friends, but ended up as rivals and antagonists.[2] Some might say that Pétain and de Gaulle both addressed the ultimate challenge of freeing France. Pétain certainly saw himself as the 'shield' protecting France, while de Gaulle represented the 'sword' which would fight for, and then consolidate, national freedom. In some senses, the two men led parallel lives; in others they were two men with extremely different political projects.

The irony of course is that de Gaulle, after piloting France towards liberation, not only became disillusioned with post-war political arrangements in France but also, during and after his presidency, became deeply unpopular. The Marshal meanwhile slid into captivity, oblivion and then death. He always retained a small band of devoted, ultra-nostalgic admirers, but for the majority of people his name became synonymous with high-level betrayal and cowardice.

Today, the many statues and commemorative plaques that grace the villages, towns and cities of France are potent reminders of the heroism of resistance, the hopes and expectations that went alongside liberation, and the awfulness and terror of the Holocaust.

But it is the statues and commemorative plaques which have not been erected that tell the real story. Visitors to the town of Vichy should not expect to see an official memorial to Pétain or Laval.

Notes

Chronology of key events

1 Compiled from A. Cobban, *A History of Modern France, Volume 3: 1871–1962* (Penguin, London, 1982); M. Collins Weitz, *Sisters in the Resistance* (Wiley, Toronto, 1995); I. Ousby, *Occupation: The Ordeal of France 1940–1944* (John Murray, London, 1998).

Introduction: background and context

1 See R. Aron, *Histoire de Vichy* (Fayard, Paris, 1954).
2 See Chapter 5.
3 R. Paxton, *Vichy France: Old Guard and New Order 1940–1944* (Columbia University Press, New York, 1982), p. xiii.
4 See Rémy, *Le 10 Mai 1940: Chronique d'une guerre perdue 2* (Editions France-Empire, Paris, 1980) and also G. Rossi-Landi, *La Drôle de guerre* (Armand Colin, Paris, 1971). J.-P. Azéma and F. Bédarida (eds), *La France des années noires* (Seuil, Paris, 1993) go one step further and use the phrase 'le cataclysme' to describe the events of 1940 (p. 95).
5 See R. Bouderon and G. Willard, *1940: de la défaite à la résistance* (Messidor, Paris, 1990), Chapter 2.
6 Cobban, op. cit., p. 258; see also W. L. Shirer, *The Collapse of the Third Republic* (Da Capo Press, New York, 1994) Book 4, pp. 519–900.
7 Cobban, op. cit., p. 177.
8 See A. Horne, *The French Army and Politics: 1870–1970* (Macmillan, London, 1984), p. 62. Horne says morale in the army was poor.
9 See Horne, op. cit., p. 54.
10 See A. Nouschi and M. Agulhon, *La France de 1914 à 1940* (Nathan, Paris, 1984), pp. 148–69.
11 Cobban, op. cit., p. 159.

I Occupation: French and Germans

1 Ousby, op. cit., p. 160.
2 For more on the Armistice see Shirer, op. cit., pp. 852–900; for different interpretations see J. Nobécourt, *Une histoire politique de l'armée (1) 1919–1942* (Seuil, Paris, 1967).
3 M. Agulhon, *The French Republic 1879–1992* (Blackwell, Oxford, 1995), p. 283.
4 H. R. Kedward, *Occupied France* (Blackwell, Oxford, 1989), p. 3.
5 M. Larkin, *France since the Popular Front* (Clarendon, Oxford, 1991) p. 82.
6 Kedward, op. cit., pp. 2–3: for three days after the fall of Dunkirk bells were rung throughout Germany.
7 See R. Thalmann, *La Mise au pas* (Fayard, Paris, 1991).
8 J. F. Sweets, *Choices in Vichy France* (OUP, New York, 1994), p. 10: the exodus also meant Strasbourg University moving en bloc to Clermont; a development which led to serious overcrowding.
9 Ousby, op. cit., p. 157.
10 Larkin, op. cit., p. 82; see also J. Defrasne, *L'Occupation allemande en France* (Presses Universitaires de France, Paris, 1985), p. 6.
11 Y. R. Simon, *The Road to Vichy 1918–1938* (University Press of America, London, 1988), p. 1.
12 Kedward (1989), op. cit., pp. 4–5.
13 See F. Bloch-Lainé and C. Gruson, *Hauts fonctionnaires sous l'occupation* (Odile Jacob, Paris, 1996) and M. O. Baruch, *Servir l'état français* (Fayard, Paris, 1997) for two investigations into how the Occupation period affected the French state. See also B. Lecornu, *Un Préfet sous l'occupation allemande* (France-Empire, Paris, 1984).
14 Franco-German Armistice, 22 June 1940, reprinted in D. Thomson (ed.), *Empire and Republic* (Harper and Row, London, 1968), pp. 357–64, Article 2.
15 Franco-German Armistice, op. cit., Article 3.
16 Simon, op. cit., p. 2.
17 Franco-German Armistice, op. cit., Article 18.
18 Franco-German Armistice, op. cit., Articles 15 and 16.
19 This term is used throughout the Armistice with full sincerity – seemingly – and also, interestingly, with a capital 'F' and 'G'.
20 Franco-German Armistice, op. cit., Article 14.
21 See H. Rousso, *Les années noires: vivre sous l'occupation* (Gallimard, Paris, 1992).
22 Sweets, op. cit., p. 7.

23 For two good case studies, see F. Bertin, *Rennes sous l'occupation* (Ouest France, Rennes, c. 1981) and B. Lecornu, op. cit.

24 Sweets, op. cit., p. 7.

25 Sweets, op. cit., p. 7.

26 H. Tint, *France since 1918* (Batsford, London, 1970), p. 95.

27 Kedward (1989), op. cit., p. 5.

28 Kedward (1989), op. cit., p. 9.

29 C. Nettelbeck (ed.), *War and Identity: The French and the Second World War* (Routledge, London, 1994): this is a good, student-friendly anthology. See Chapters 3 and 4.

30 Defrasne (1985), op. cit., p. 45.

31 Defrasne (1985), op. cit., pp. 45–61.

32 Cobban, op. cit., p. 193.

33 See H. Michel, *Paris allemand* (Albin Michel, Paris, 1981), Chapters 6 and 7.

34 See Ousby, op. cit., pp. 124–5.

35 Collins Weitz, op. cit., p. 39. See also p. 42: there were masses of black market dealings and, in time, trials for 'infractions of rationing regulations'. Sweets, op. cit., p. 8, p. 11 and p. 14 sums up the southern-zone situation: it was even worse than that which existed in the occupied northern zone.

36 Sweets, op. cit., p. 21.

37 Sweets, op. cit., p. 21.

38 For a provocative regional study of the Occupation and its effects see T. Todorov and A. Jacquet, *Guerre et paix sous l'occupation* (Arléa, Paris, 1996).

39 See A. Beltran, R. Frank and H. Rousso, *La Vie des enterprises sous l'occupation* (Belin, Paris, 1994) for an excellent survey.

40 Ousby, op. cit., pp. 130–1.

41 Agulhon, op. cit., p. 293.

42 Pem (1944) reproduced in Agulhon, op. cit., p. 294.

43 See Sweets, op. cit., p. 23 and pp. 24–8, and Cobban, op. cit., p. 193.

44 Cobban, op. cit., p. 193; Agulhon, op. cit., pp. 295–6.

45 See S. de Beauvoir, *The Prime of Life* (Penguin, London, 1960), p. 458 and p. 464.

46 Michel (1981), op. cit., Chapters 6 and 7.

47 Michel (1981), op. cit.

48 H. Michel, B. Mirkine-Guetzévitch and D. Mayer (eds), *La France sous l'occupation* (Presses Universitaires de France, Paris, 1959), p. 69.

49 Ousby, op. cit., p. 121.

50 See Defrasne (1985), op. cit., pp. 111–16.

51 De Beauvoir, op. cit., p. 475.

52 On films see F. Garçon, *De Blum à Petain* (Cerf, Paris, 1984).

53 Agulhon, op. cit., pp. 284–5. The intellectual and artistic life was 'upset' by the Occupation; Agulhon plays down the renaissance. See *Hidden Hands* documentary, 'Art and culture under the Occupation', Channel 4, 1996.

54 Agulhon, op. cit., pp. 284–5.

55 'Art and culture under the Occupation', op. cit.

56 P. Burrin, *Living with Defeat* (Seuil, London, 1991), p. 296.

57 Burrin, op. cit., pp. 296–9.

58 Agulhon, op. cit., p. 283.

59 H. Diamond, 'The everyday experience of women during the Second World War in the Toulouse region' in M. Scriven and P. Wagstaff (eds), *War and Society in Twentieth Century France* (Berg, Oxford, 1991), p. 50.

60 Collins Weitz, op. cit., pp. 23–4.

61 Ousby, op. cit., pp. 154–5.

62 After the war though, the depiction changed. From then on France was generally personified in strong and powerful male figures.

63 Ousby, op. cit., pp. 154–5 and p. 160.

64 Ousby, op. cit., pp. 154–5; see also Vercors, *The Silence of the Sea*, J. W. Brown and L. D. Stokes (eds), (Berg, Oxford, 1993).

65 See *'Allo 'Allo* (a BBC television comedy broadcast throughout the 1980s and 1990s) for an *extremely* stereotypical view of the German occupiers.

66 See Defrasne (1985), op. cit., pp. 76–86; see also J. Delperrie de Bayac, *Histoire de la milice 2: Les assassins de l'ordre* (Fayard, Paris, 1969).

67 Vercors, op. cit.

68 See de Beauvoir, op. cit., pp. 446–52.

69 De Beauvoir, op. cit., p. 447.

70 Sweets, op. cit., p. 15.

71 Agulhon, op. cit., p. 283.

72 Agulhon, op. cit., p. 283.

73 J. Adler, *The Jews of Paris and the Final Solution* (OUP, Oxford, 1989), p. 32.

74 Adler, op. cit., p. 32: as we saw in Chapter 1.

75 Hence the title of Ousby's book (op. cit.).

76 Ousby, op. cit., p. 161.

77 Collins Weitz, op. cit., p. 27 (my italics).

78 J.-P. Sartre, *Paris sous l'occupation* (Gallimard, Paris, 1949); see also Sweets, op. cit., p. 14.

79 Sartre, op. cit.

80 Collins Weitz, op. cit., p. 41.

81 Sweets, op. cit., p. 6.

82 Ousby, op. cit., p. 123.

83 Ousby, op. cit., p. 138.
84 Sartre, op. cit.
85 The cartoon appeared in the newspaper, *La France au travail*.
86 Sweets, op. cit., p. 28.
87 Kedward (1989), op. cit., p. 4.
88 Larkin, op. cit., p. 103.

2 Vichy and collaboration: from the National Revolution to Hitler's revolution

1 Speech of 11 October 1940 in S. M. Osgood (ed.), *The Fall of France, 1940* (Heath, London, 1965), pp. 12–13.
2 Vichy tourist poster for 'LE NOUVEAU PALAIS DES CONGRÈS OPÉRA'.
3 See P. Péllissier, *Philippe Pétain* (Hachette, Paris, 1980), pp. 11–212 for Pétain's pre-1940 life and career. It is also significant that the subtitle to Nobécourt's book on the French army (op. cit.) is '*De Pétain à Pétain*'.
4 P. Claudel in J. S. McLelland (ed.), *The French Right* (Jonathan Cape, London, 1961), pp. 18–20.
5 Contemporary reworking of the Lord's prayer.
6 P. Milza, *Fascisme français* (Flammarion, Paris, 1987), p. 231; J.-F. Sirinelli (ed.), *Les Droites françaises* (Gallimard, Paris, 1992), p. 565.
7 P. Birnbaum, *La France aux français* (Seuil, Paris, 1993), pp. 166–7.
8 See J. Isorni, *Le Condamné de la citadelle* (Flammarion, Paris, 1982).
9 N. Atkin, *Pétain* (Longman, London, 1998).
10 We should note here, as R. Rémond does in *The Right Wing in France* (University of Pennsylvania Press, Philadelphia, 1971, p. 309) that 'Vichy' should not be combined with, or viewed as the same thing as, 'collaboration'; indeed, 'they had lots of quarrels'.
11 M. Anderson, *Conservative Politics in France* (Allen and Unwin, London, 1974), p. 69.
12 P. Goubert, *The Course of French History* (Routledge, London, 1991), p. 295.
13 See F.-G. Dreyfus, *Histoire de Vichy* (Perrin, Paris, 1990) for an in-depth study of the regime and the various factions at play within the government.
14 R. Griffiths, *Pétain* (Constable, London, 1970), p. 253.
15 R. Griffin, *The Nature of Fascism* (Routledge, London, 1994), p. 135. See W. Laqueur (ed.), *Fascism: A Reader's Guide* (Penguin, London, 1982), pp. 304–5, for more on this debate.

16 Larkin, op. cit., p. 90; Rémond, op. cit., pp. 309–11 and pp. 313–14; see also Griffiths, op. cit., p. 254.

17 A. Werth, *France 1940–1955* (Robert Hale, London, 1957), p. 43.

18 See M. Ferro, *Pétain* (Fayard, Paris, 1987), pp. 215–88: note in particular the influence of Salazar on Pétain, pp. 215–17.

19 Anderson, op. cit., p. 68.

20 Griffiths, op. cit., p. 257. For more on Vichy and freemasons, see D. Rossignol, *Vichy et les francs-maçons* (Lattès, Paris, 1981).

21 Werth (1957), op. cit., p. 36.

22 Pétain, 'Message to the French People, 11 October 1940' as reprinted in D. Thomson (ed.), *Empire and Republic* (Harper and Row, London, 1968).

23 Griffiths, op. cit., p. 265.

24 Werth (1957), op. cit., p. 37.

25 Anderson, op. cit., p. 69.

26 Sirinelli, op. cit., p. 569.

27 Pétain, 'Message to the French People', op. cit.

28 Rémond, op. cit., p. 314.

29 G. Wright, *France in Modern Times* (Norton, London, 1995), p. 385.

30 One Vichy poster showed two houses standing side by side: one decrepit (representing the old Republic) and one solid and in fine health (representing the Vichy regime).

31 Larkin, op. cit., p. 94.

32 See G. Wright, *Rural Revolution in France* (OUP, London, 1964).

33 The Vichy regime came to adopt the *francisque* – an axe-like implement used in ancient Gaul – as its main symbol.

34 Wright (1964), op. cit., p. 76.

35 Wright (1964), op. cit., p. 91: the life of the Vichy regime was short; thus, the argument is that it had a minimal impact.

36 Caziot was a key agriculture minister. See Wright (1964), op. cit., p. 79.

37 Wright (1964), op. cit., p. 87, says the 'Vichy era temporarily slowed (the) flow of the rural élite toward the cities'.

38 Griffiths, op. cit., p. 259: Vichy mistrusted capitalism and socialism.

39 Griffiths, op. cit., p. 261.

40 Werth (1957), op. cit., p. 37.

41 See J. F. McMillan, *Twentieth Century France* (Edward Arnold, London, 1992), p. 139; see also Werth (1957), op. cit., p. 53, and Milza, op. cit., p. 234. For a full discussion see J.-P. Le Crom, *Syndicats nous voilà! Vichy et le corporatisme* (Atelier, Paris, 1995), pp. 105–66.

42 Werth (1957), op. cit., p. 36.

43 Larkin, op. cit., p. 95.

44 Rémond, op. cit., p. 317. On p. 311 Rémond suggests that the 'liberal

right' was really only in evidence in the economic sphere; for the rest of the time, it is claimed, the fascist and conservative right was in the ascendancy at Vichy. See also Chapter 5.

45 Many commentators actually point to a continuity running through the *nataliste* policies of the Popular Front and Vichy.

46 A. Copley, *Sexual Moralities in France* (Routledge, London, 1992), p. 200.

47 Larkin, op. cit., pp. 90–1.

48 Copley, op. cit., pp. 203–4 .

49 Vichy poster c. 1941.

50 Like Frederic Le Play: Rémond, op. cit., p. 315.

51 Copley, op. cit., p. 201.

52 See W. D. Halls, *Politics, Society and Christianity in Vichy France* (Berg, Oxford, 1995), pp. 269–310; see also B. Comte, *Une utopie combattante* (Fayard, Paris, 1991).

53 Larkin, op. cit., pp. 91–2: 'Youth groups never reached fascist style'; See also Milza, op. cit., 238–40, and Copley, op. cit.: Vichy youth groups seemed to have more in common with English public schools than fascist youth movements.

54 Vichy poster c. 1940–1.

55 See P. Drieu la Rochelle in Osgood, op. cit., p. 50.

56 Rémond, op. cit., p. 316; Larkin, op. cit., p. 93.

57 Halls, op. cit., p. 182.

58 N. Atkin and F. Tallett, *Religion, Society and Politics in France since 1789* (Hambledon, London, 1991), pp. 165–6; Copley, op. cit., p. 201.

59 For more depth on this, see Halls, op. cit., throughout.

60 Vichy poster c. 1940–41.

61 S. J. Lee, *The European Dictatorships 1918–1945* (Routledge, London, 1984), pp. 296–7.

62 This phrase has come to describe the relationships between French women and German men during the war.

63 R. Price, *A Concise History of France* (CUP, Cambridge, 1993), p. 258.

64 J. Defrasne, *Histoire de la collaboration* (Presses Universitaires de France, Paris, 1982), pp. 55–88.

65 See P. Ory, *Les Collaborateurs 1940–1945* (Seuil, Paris, 1976), pp. 36–53.

66 See Péllissier, op. cit., pp. 235–51; see also F. Delpla, *Montoire* (Albin Michel, Paris, 1996).

67 Defrasne (1982), op. cit., pp. 118–21.

68 On Montoire see P. Laval, *The Unpublished Diary of Pierre Laval* (Falcon, London, 1948), pp. 48–52 and pp. 62–6.

69 For more on the 1930s see F. Braudel's Foreword in *Les années trente de la crise à la guerre* (Seuil, Paris, 1983).

70 Paxton, op. cit., p. 51.

71 See Laval, op. cit., pp. 70–9.

72 Laval, op. cit., p. 17.

73 D. Bair, *Simone de Beauvoir: A Biography* (Vintage, London, 1991), pp. 295–6.

74 Adler, op. cit., p. 15.

75 Cobban, op. cit., p. 184; P. Webster, *Pétain's Crime* (Papermac, London, 1994), op. cit., p. 3.

76 See Adler, op. cit., p. 25 – Vichy usually acquiesced. M. Marrus and R. Paxton, *Vichy France and the Jews* (Stanford University Press, Stanford, 1995), p. xv, explain this situation.

77 Griffiths, op. cit., p. 263.

78 S. Zuccotti, *The Holocaust, the French, and the Jews* (Basic Books, New York, 1999), p. 4.

79 See Larkin, op. cit., p. 101, and Marrus and Paxton, op. cit., pp. 75–119.

80 See Adler, op. cit., Chapter 2.

81 See Zuccotti, op. cit., pp. 51–64, Marrus and Paxton, op. cit., pp. 3–5.

82 General point made by P. Hyman, *From Dreyfus to Vichy* (New York, Columbia University Press, 1979). For more on anti-semitism in the 1930s see P. J. Kingston, *Anti-semitism in France during the 1930s* (University of Hull, Hull, 1983). See also Marrus and Paxton, op. cit., pp. 25–71 and Zuccotti, op. cit., pp. 7–30. Marrus and Paxton conclude that French anti-semitism was homegrown.

83 See R. S. Wistrich, *Anti-Semitism* (Mandarin, London, 1992), pp. 126–44.

84 See Adler, op. cit., p. 15; see also Marrus and Paxton, op. cit., pp. 3–21.

85 See Marrus and Paxton, op. cit., pp. 19–20.

86 Price, op. cit., p. 260.

87 Cobban, op. cit., p. 184.

88 Larkin, op. cit., p. 100.

89 McMillan, op. cit., p. 138.

90 Price, op. cit., p. 261.

91 See Laval, op. cit., pp. 104–21. For some interesting thoughts on Laval see M. Marrus, 'Vichy et les enfants juif' in *Études sur la France de 1939 à nos jours* (Seuil, Paris, 1985).

92 See Laval, op. cit., pp. 53–61.

93 For more on the response to Vichy's Jewish policy, see Adler, op. cit., Chapters 3 and 4.

94 Ory (1984), op. cit., p. 11.

95 See G. Hirschfeld and P. Marsh, *Collaboration in France* (Berg, Oxford, 1989), pp. 47–71.

96 P. Ory (ed.), *La France allemande: paroles du collaborationnisme français (1933–1945)* (Gallimard/Julliard, Paris, 1977).

97 McMillan, op. cit., p. 142. See M. Déat, *Mémoires politiques* (Denoël,

Paris, 1989); rather pertinently, the second part of this book is entitled 'Le combat pour l'impossible'.

98 Werth (1957), op. cit., p. 125.
99 McMillan, op. cit., pp. 142–3; see also the interesting case of Simon Sabiani in P. Jankowski, *Communism and Collaboration: Simon Sabiani and Politics in Marseille 1919–44* (Yale University Press, New Haven and London, 1989).
100 Sirinelli, op. cit., p. 568.
101 See Ory (1977), op. cit., pp. 168–235.
102 Anderson, op. cit., pp. 66–75.
103 Milza, op. cit., p. 230 and pp. 235–7.
104 Rémond, op. cit., pp. 316–17; Griffiths, op. cit., p. 264, agrees: the claim is that there was nothing further than the National Revolution from fascism; Webster, op. cit., p. 45, talks about the 'air of ridicule' at Vichy for four years.

3 Resistance: internal and external

1 De Gaulle 'Message to the people of France', as quoted in D. Cook, *Charles de Gaulle: A Biography* (Putnam, London, 1983).
2 F. Bédarida, 'De Gaulle and the Resistance 1940–1944' in H. Gough and J. Horne (eds), *De Gaulle and Twentieth Century France* (Edward Arnold, London, 1994), p. 20, alludes to this.
3 See F. Knight, *The French Resistance 1940–4* (Lawrence and Wishart, London, 1975), pp. 68–71. The red, white and blue colours were particularly prominent in the large-scale university demonstration of 11 November 1940.
4 P. Williams, *Politics in Post-War France* (Longmans, London, 1958), p. 114, argues that the arrival of de Gaulle's wife and children gave the Free French leader the confidence to 'run up his true colours'.
5 See Bédarida, op. cit., p. 23 and H. Noguères, M. Degliame-Fouché and J.-L. Vigier, *Histoire de la résistance en France de 1940 à 1945, Vol. 1 June 1940–June 1941* (Robert Laffont, Paris, 1967).
6 F.-G. Dreyfus, *Histoire de la résistance* (Fallois, Paris, 1996), p. 237.
7 For an interesting angle on resistance (and the way in which France was liberated), see A. Debon, *La Mission helmsman* (Harmattan, Paris, 1997).
8 See Ousby, op. cit., p. 210 and p. 245; and also Agulhon, op. cit., p. 288.
9 H. R. Kedward, *Resistance in Vichy France* (OUP, Oxford, 1978), pp. 185–6.
10 See I. Higgins, 'France, soil and language: some Resistance poems by Luc

Berimont and Jean Marcenac' in H. R. Kedward and R. Austin, *Vichy France and Resistance* (Croom Helm, London, 1985), p. 219.

11 A. Shennan, *Rethinking France* (OUP, Oxford, 1989), p. 35.

12 L. Lévy, *France is a Democracy* (Victor Gollancz, Paris, 1942), p. 141.

13 See Ousby, op. cit., pp. 219–20.

14 Kedward (1978), op. cit., pp. 126–8.

15 S. Hawes, 'The individual and the Resistance community in France' in S. Hawes and R. White, *Resistance in Europe 1939–45* (Penguin, London, 1976), p. 118 and p. 132.

16 Interestingly, Hawes, op. cit., says the tendency was to say 'I' during the Resistance period and 'We' during the Liberation (see pp. 118–19). Refer to C. Andrews on 'Myths and memories of World War II', BBC2, 1996.

17 A. Cady, 'Discourses of Resistance' in M. Scriven and P. Wagstaff (eds), *War and Society in Twentieth Century France* (Berg, Oxford, 1991), p. 250; this is reflected in Shennan (1989), op. cit., p. 50.

18 Kedward (1978), op. cit., p. 230.

19 Shennan (1989), op. cit., p. 37.

20 Werth (1957), op. cit., p. 156.

21 H. Lottman, *The People's Anger: Justice and Revenge in Post-Liberation France* (Hutchinson, London, 1986), p. 21.

22 Werth (1957), op. cit., p. 133.

23 Hawes, op. cit., p. 133; Werth (1957), op. cit., p. 138.

24 Kedward (1978), op. cit., p. 229; see also A. Beevor and A. Cooper, *Paris after the Liberation* (Hamish Hamilton, London, 1994), p. 26.

25 Hawes, op. cit., p. 122.

26 See Kedward (1978), op. cit., for some fascinating profiles.

27 See Beevor and Cooper, op. cit., Chapter 3.

28 This 'heroism' can be seen in the many picture-book-style life-stories of de Gaulle which appeared after the war.

29 Vercors, op. cit.

30 Vercors, op. cit., p. 73.

31 Celebrated resistance individuals include Colonel Fabien (see Ousby, op. cit., p. 223) and Gerhard Heller (see Lottman [1986], op. cit., pp. 174–9). For significant personal memoirs see L. Joxe, *Victoires sur la nuit* (Flammarion, Paris, 1981) and C. Chevrillon, *Une résistance ordinaire* (Félin, Paris, 1999).

32 See L. Allen, 'Resistance and the Catholic Church in France', in S. Hawes and R. White, *Resistance in Europe: 1939–45* (Penguin, London, 1976) p. 81 and p. 87.

33 See C. Andrieu, 'Les résistantes, perspectives de recherche' in A. Prost (ed.), *La Résistance, une histoire sociale* (Les Editions de l'Atelier, Paris, 1997), pp. 85–9.

34 See early posters of the Resistance (also note the presence of 'Michelle' in *'Allo 'Allo*).

35 See M. Collins Weitz, op. cit., pp. 7–8.

36 Cady, op. cit., p. 251.

37 Ousby, op. cit., p. 231, Agulhon, op. cit., p. 289.

38 Ousby, op. cit., p. 216.

39 Burrin, op. cit., pp. 192–3.

40 On art see Knight, op. cit., p. 147 and p. 149; on literature: see Cady, op. cit., p. 256, Knight, op. cit., p. 147 and p. 149, Higgins, op. cit., and E. Tolansky, 'Les cahiers du silence' in H. R. Kedward and R. Austin, *Vichy France and the Resistance*, op. cit.

41 Kedward (1978), op. cit., p. 231.

42 See H. Michel and B. Markine-Guetzévitch, *Les Ideés politiques et sociales de la résistance* (Presses Universitaires de France, Paris, 1954).

43 Ousby, op. cit., pp. 212–13.

44 See Andrieu, op. cit., p. 83.

45 Lévy, op. cit., pp. 141–3.

46 R. Cole, *A Traveller's History of France* (Windrush, Moreton-in-Marsh, 1996), p. 163.

47 A. Werth, *De Gaulle* (Penguin, London, 1969), p. 101: 'Free France' became 'Fighting France' (*'La France combattante'*) from 29 July onwards.

48 See Shennan (1989), op. cit., Chapter 3 on organisation, committees, and the nature of Free France in exile.

49 Lévy, op. cit., p. 141.

50 See Cook, op. cit.

51 Werth (1969), op. cit., p. 104.

52 See H. Amouroux, *Le 18 Juin 40* (Fayard, Paris, 1990) for a full discussion of the significance of de Gaulle's radio broadcast.

53 See cartoon from the French press in which Germany is depicted as a large eagle and the Resistance is depicted as a cluster of eggs fighting back.

54 De Gaulle, *War Memoirs*, Volume 1 (Collins, London, 1959), p. 87.

55 Beevor and Cooper, op. cit., p. 25, depict de Gaulle as a 'regent'; see also Werth (1969), op. cit., pp. 101–61.

56 De Gaulle, op. cit., p. 89 and p. 92.

57 A. Hartley, *Gaullism* (Routledge and Kegan Paul, London, 1972), p. 52. See also Agulhon, op. cit., p. 264.

58 See A. Shennan, *De Gaulle* (Longman, London, 1993), p. 16; Bédarida argues, in addition, that the three main sections into which de Gaulle's memoirs are divided – 'Call', 'Unity' and 'Salvation' – are remarkably accurate pointers to the essence of Gaullist wartime activity.

59 See Knight, op. cit., 'The Free French in London', Chapter 9.
60 See Williams, op. cit., pp. 213–14; the Algiers episode revealed serious tensions in the relationship between France and Britain/the USA. Giraud – de Gaulle's 'rival' in Algiers – was the symbol of this tension. See also H. Michel, *Histoire de la France libre* (Presses Universitaires de France, Paris, 1963).
61 See also Chapter 10 in S. Hazareesingh, *Political Traditions in Modern France* (OUP, Oxford, 1996), pp. 261–87.
62 J. Jackson, *De Gaulle* (Cardinal, London, 1990), pp. 10–24.
63 Hartley, op. cit., p. 93.
64 See Williams, op. cit., p. 190.
65 Jackson, op. cit., p. 12.
66 For more on de Gaulle's writings see A. Pedley, *As Mighty as the Sword: A Study of the Writings of Charles de Gaulle* (Elm Bank, Exeter, 1996).
67 Hartley, op. cit., p. 53.
68 Bédarida, op. cit., p. 27.
69 For more on the 'legitimacy' issue, see A. Laurens, *Les Rivaux de Charles de Gaulle: La bataille de la légitimité en France de 1940 à 1944* (Robert Laffont, Paris, 1977).
70 Shennan (1993), op. cit., pp. 16–38.
71 The FN stood for '*La lutte pour la libération et l'independence de la France*'.
72 See L. Douzou, *La Désobedience: histoire du mouvement libération-sud* (Odile Jacob, Paris, 1995).
73 Larkin, op. cit., p. 108–10. For an in-depth study see D. Veillon, *Le Franc-Tireur* (Flammarion, Paris, 1977). See also J.-P. Levy, *Memoires d'un franc-tireur* (Complexe, Paris, 1998).
74 *Franc-Tireur*, via its newspaper, *Témoignage Chrétien* (9 May 1945) claimed to be '*à l'avant-garde de la République*'. The full title of the newspaper was *Courier Français du Témoignage Chrétien – Lien du Front de Resistance Spirituelle*.
75 See Larkin, op. cit., p. 108; MUR stood for *Mouvement Unifié de la Renaissance*. Its slogan was '*Il reste à libérer la République*'.
76 See O. Wieviorka, *Une certaine idée de la résistance* (Seuil, Paris, 1995) for a discussion of intra-resistance relations.
77 For a broader discussion, see H. R. Kedward, 'Behind the polemics: French communists and Resistance 1939–41' in S. Hawes and R. White, *Resistance in Europe: 1939–45* (Penguin, London, 1976); see also Ousby, op. cit., pp. 204–6 and Agulhon, op. cit., pp. 290–3.
78 Cobban, op. cit., p. 190.
79 Werth (1957), op. cit., p. 179.
80 See Knight, op. cit., pp. 62–7.

81 Knight, op. cit., pp. 62–7.
82 See A. Kriegel and S. Courtois, *Eugen Fried* (Seuil, Paris, 1997), p. 370.
83 Cobban, op. cit., p. 196.
84 See Allen, op. cit., p. 78, for more on the PCF and the catholics; Beevor and Cooper, op. cit., p. 28, for more on the PCF and the Gaullists.
85 For a provocative essay on the question of the French socialists and the Resistance, see *Études sur la France de 1939 à nos jours*, op. cit., pp. 138–53; see also P. Guidoni and R. Verdier (eds), *Les Socialistes en résistance* (Seli Arslan, Paris, 1999).
86 McMillan, op. cit., p. 149; see also G. Chauvy, *Histoire secrète de l'occupation* (Payot, Paris, 1991).
87 See H. R. Kedward, 'The Maquis: whose history?' in M. Scriven and P. Wagstaff (eds), *War and Society in Twentieth Century France* (Berg, Oxford, 1991) for more on this; see also Kedward (1985), op. cit., for help in understanding the Maquis (especially p. 236). Maquisards are equated to 'bandits'. Important inroads are also made by H. R. Kedward, *In Search of the Maquis: Rural Resistance in Southern France 1942–44* (Oxford, Clarendon, 1994).
88 Kedward (1991), op. cit.
89 For more on this see Ousby, op. cit., pp. 254–5. He refers to the Maquis as 'outlaws'; he also comments on the naming of the Maquis' units: they took the names of wild animals rather than abstract concepts (p. 260).
90 For a study of the Maquis in La Creuse, see M. Parrotin, *Le Temps du Maquis* (2nd edition, 1981). For a more general study, see D. Schoenbrun, *Maquis* (Robert Hale, London, 1990).
91 Ousby, op. cit., pp. 257–8.
92 35–40 per cent of Ariege maquisards were STO runaways (Kedward 1985, op. cit., pp. 232–5). Kedward also points out (p. 233) that there were very few maquisards before the STO; before this it was a predominantly urban phenomenon. See also Allen, op. cit., p. 91. It was 'not sinful to disobey'; therefore there were STO–maquisard 'transfers'.
93 Burrin, op. cit., p. 186.
94 For more on the Maquis see H. Michel, *Histoire de la résistance en France* (Presses Universitaires de France, Paris, 1965), pp. 91–101.
95 See Knight, op. cit., on the Maquis, Chapter 15; see also Kedward (1991), op. cit., and Kedward (1985), op. cit.
96 See Lottman, op. cit., pp. 21–31 and pp. 32–43.
97 Bédarida, op. cit., p. 22.
98 Larkin, op. cit., p. 109.
99 See Michel (1963), op. cit., pp. 56–74.
100 See Agulhon, op. cit., p. 286.
101 Bédarida, op. cit., pp. 20–5.

102 Jackson, op. cit., p. 19.
103 See Agulhon, op. cit., pp. 297–9.
104 De Gaulle, op. cit., p. 93.
105 Werth (1969), op. cit., p. 123.
106 Jackson, op. cit., p. 15.
107 Beevor and Cooper, op. cit., p. 31; the Allies' internecine struggle was more passionate than their struggle versus Hitler (see Agulhon, op. cit., pp. 264–5); see also J. Fenby, *On the Brink* (Little, Brown, London, 1998), p. 268.
108 For more on Syria and Dakar see Hartley, op. cit., pp. 60–3.
109 Werth (1969), op. cit., p. 161.
110 Shennan (1989), op. cit., p. 34, pp. 40–2 and p. 52.
111 Ousby, op. cit., p. 215.
112 Cady, op. cit., pp. 249–50; Shennan (1989), op. cit., p. 43.
113 See Andrews, op. cit.
114 Dreyfus (1996), op. cit., pp. 585–7.
115 Ousby, op. cit., p. 209.
116 Kedward (1989), op. cit., p. 80. Chapter 4 of this book is a good general survey of the Resistance.

4 Liberation: freedom, hope and relief

1 H. R. Kedward in H. R. Kedward and N. Wood (eds), *The Liberation of France* (Berg, Oxford, 1995), p. 3.
2 McMillan, op. cit., p. 149.
3 Beevor and Cooper, op. cit., p. 59.
4 Kedward and Wood, op. cit., Part II and Part IV.
5 McMillan, op. cit., p. 149.
6 For more on this day see C. Mauriac, *The Other De Gaulle* (Angus and Robertson, London, 1973). This book offers fascinating insights into de Gaulle in the period 1944–6.
7 See Beevor and Cooper, op. cit., Chapter 5, 'Liberated Paris', pp. 58–69; they definitely see the Liberation as being about one day – 26 August 1944. See also J. Lacouture, *De Gaulle: The Rebel 1890–1944* (Norton, London, 1990): he views the Liberation as 'The Consecration'.
8 Taken from Cobban, op. cit., pp. 258–9. See also Kedward (1989), op. cit., Chapter 5, pp. 61–80: a good general survey.
9 See Kedward's Introduction in Kedward and Wood, op. cit., pp. 1–2.
10 'Premature' or 'abortive' liberations – see Kedward in Kedward and Wood, op. cit., p. 1.

11 Kedward and Wood, op. cit., p. ix; see also Kedward, p. 2, in Kedward and Wood, op. cit.

12 Ousby, op. cit., p. 278.

13 Knight, op. cit., pp. 209–10.

14 Larkin, op. cit., p. 114.

15 H. Footitt and J. Simmonds, 'The politics of liberation: France 1943–1945' in M. Scriven and P. Wagstaff (eds), *War and Society in Twentieth Century France* (Berg, Oxford, 1991), pp. 100–5 and p. 108. The Allies actually needed de Gaulle and the French to take over; they would have been 'in the soup' otherwise. See also Kedward (1989), op. cit., p. 78.

16 Kedward in Kedward and Wood, op. cit., pp. 2–3.

17 Footitt and Simmonds, op. cit., pp. 96–7 and p. 99.

18 Jackson, op. cit., p. 21.

19 See Cook, op. cit., pp. 221–46, for a good narrative account of de Gaulle and the Liberation.

20 Ousby, op. cit., p. 294.

21 See Shennan (1989), op. cit., pp. 55–64.

22 Ousby, op. cit., p. 298.

23 Jackson, op. cit., p. 21 and Ousby, op. cit., p. 280: the new Liberation currency looked like US dollars.

24 Price, op. cit., p. 267; see also McMillan, op. cit., p. 150.

25 Jackson, op. cit., p. 22.

26 McMillan, op. cit., p. 150.

27 Jackson, op. cit., p. 23.

28 See Footitt and Simmonds, op. cit., p. 102.

29 Kedward (1989), op. cit., p. 71.

30 McMillan, op. cit., p. 150.

31 Kedward in Kedward and Wood, op. cit., p. 3.

32 Footitt and Simmonds, op. cit., p. 99.

33 See A. Kaspi, *La Libération de la France* (Perrin, Paris, 1995).

34 S. Barber, *Weapons of Liberation* (Faber and Faber, London, 1996), p. 23.

35 See Price, op. cit., pp. 267–302.

36 Kedward in Kedward and Wood, op. cit., p. 6, talks about Jean-Marie Guillon.

37 A poster issued by the GPRF *Secrétariat Général à l'Information* in August 1944.

38 Kedward in Kedward and Wood, op. cit, p. 9.

39 Larkin, op. cit., p. 115; McMillan, op. cit., p. 150.

40 Price, op. cit., pp. 267–302.

41 Kedward's Introduction in Kedward and Wood, op. cit., p. 3.

42 Kedward (1989), op. cit., pp. 77–8.

43 Posters issued by the GPRF *Secrétariat Général à l'Information* in August 1944. This general tone was also echoed in the press, e.g. *Ce Soir* special supplement, 14 July 1945, '*La leçon de 1789*', where revolutionary and Liberation symbols were interwoven.
44 Barber, op. cit., pp. 1–2.
45 Barber, op. cit., p. 2.
46 Barber, op. cit., p. 3 and throughout chapter.
47 See J.-P. Rioux, *The Fourth Republic 1944–1958* (CUP, Cambridge, 1989), pp. 29–42.
48 Ousby, op. cit., p. 303.
49 See Ousby, op. cit., p. 275; see also *Études sur la France de 1939 à nos jours*, op. cit., pp. 162–4.
50 Ousby, op. cit., p. 299.
51 Barber, op. cit., p. 19.
52 Beevor and Cooper, op. cit., p. 179.
53 Ousby, op. cit., p. 303.
54 Each and every author seems to have a different estimate of the scale of the devastation.
55 McMillan, op. cit., p. 152.
56 Ousby, op. cit., p. 303.
57 The French authorities' posters in the mid-1940s.
58 J. Dalloz, *La France de la libération* (Presses Universitaires de France, Paris, 1983), pp. 35–47.
59 Footitt and Simmonds, op. cit., p. 109.
60 Kedward (1989), op. cit., pp. 76–8.
61 This was born in 1947.

5 Legacy: an era still alive

1 H. Rousso, *The Vichy Syndrome* (Harvard University Press, Cambridge, Mass., 1994), p. 1.
2 R. Gildea, *France since 1945* (OUP, Oxford, 1996), p. 56.
3 Beevor and Cooper, op. cit., p. ix.
4 A. Maurois, *A History of France* (Jonathan Cape, London, 1960), p. 507.
5 *Independent on Sunday*, 24 March 1991.
6 See P. Ouston, *France in the Twentieth Century* (Macmillan, London, 1972), pp. 222–5.
7 A. Morris, *Collaboration and Resistance Reviewed* (Berg, New York, 1992), p. 1.
8 H. Lottman, *The Left Bank* (Halo, San Francisco, 1991), p. 238.
9 Maurois, op. cit., p. 510.

10 Williams, op. cit., p. 11.

11 Cobban, op. cit., p. 201.

12 Gildea, op. cit., p. 59.

13 Gildea, op. cit., p. 58.

14 Cobban, op. cit., pp. 214–15.

15 Williams, op. cit., p. 14.

16 Price, op. cit., p. 274; McMillan, op. cit., p. 154.

17 J. Corbett, *Through French Windows* (University of Michigan Press, Michigan, 1997), pp. 22–3.

18 See Rioux, op. cit., Chapter 11, pp. 170–87 for more on the post-war economic construction. See also J. A. Huston, *Across the Face of France* (University Press of America, London, 1984), Chapter 15.

19 Rioux, op. cit., p. 170.

20 Huston, op. cit., p. 228.

21 Corbett, op. cit., p. 368; see also J. Ardagh, *France in the New Century* (Viking, London, 1999), pp. 62–6. See J. Monnet, *Memoirs* (Collins, London, 1978) – especially Part 2, 'A Time for Unity'.

22 For a fuller discussion see A. G. Hargreaves (ed.), *Immigration in Post-War France* (Methuen, London, 1987).

23 Collins Weitz, op. cit., pp. 286–307. For a very general reader-friendly anthology see C. Laubier (ed.), *The Condition of Women in France: 1945 to the Present* (Routledge, London, 1990): the opening four chapters.

24 Jackson, op. cit., pp. 66–7.

25 Jackson, op. cit., p. 54.

26 Cobban, op. cit., p. 215.

27 Cobban, op. cit., p. 216.

28 Jackson, op. cit., p. 73. See A. W. Deporte, *De Gaulle's Foreign Policy 1944–1946* (Harvard University Press, Cambridge, Mass., 1968) for more on de Gaulle's foreign policy generally.

29 See Rioux, op. cit., Chapter 9, pp. 133–50 ('France under the American umbrella'); see also Tint, pp. 105–18 ('France in 1949 seemed to have lost faith in herself'). See also Shennan (1989), op. cit., p. 69, and Huston, op. cit., pp. 97–158: the case study is Orleans; the general point is made in these pages.

30 R. Kuisel, *Seducing the French* (University of California, Berkeley, 1996), p. 18. The historian is Pierre Nora.

31 Today, in their differing ways, Chirac and Le Pen both exhibit a strong anti-Americanism. On the right and extreme right, there seems to be an in-bred hostility to all things American: from the Internet to Euro-Disney.

32 The ultimate guide is Rioux, op. cit.

33 Cobban, op. cit., pp. 205–7.

34 See Williams, op. cit., p. 17. For de Gaulle there was 'exasperation with the quarrels of the parties'.
35 Williams, op. cit., p. 16.
36 Cobban, op. cit., p. 214.
37 N. Hewlett, *Modern French Politics* (Polity, Cambridge, 1998), p. 36.
38 Hewlett, op. cit., p. 50, calls it France's 'political exceptionalism'.
39 See, for example, M. Winock, *Nationalisme, antisémitisme et fascisme en France* (Seuil, Paris, 1990), Chapter 10: 'De Gaulle dernier nationaliste', pp. 416–35.
40 See B. Crozier, *De Gaulle: The Statesman* (Methuen, London, 1973).
41 Rémond, op. cit., p. 318.
42 L. Cheles, R. Ferguson and M. Vaughan (eds), *Neo-Fascism in Europe* (Longman, London, 1991), p. 214.
43 M. Winock, *Histoire de l'Éxtrême droite en France* (Seuil, Paris, 1994), p. 216.
44 Winock (1994), op. cit., p. 215.
45 Winock (1994), op. cit., p. 215.
46 Milza, op. cit., p. 277 – see also p. 295 (the same point is made); colonial conflict and the revolt of small businessmen aided the return of the Vichy and collaborationist generation. See also Anderson, op. cit., p. 275.
47 Cheles *et al.*, op. cit., p. 215.
48 Winock (1994), op. cit., Chapter 7, p. 215.
49 For example, Poujade himself who had Vichy associations in his early life though he later joined the Resistance.
50 Rémond, op. cit., p. 323.
51 McMillan, op. cit., p. 152.
52 Anderson, op. cit., p. 273: many Vichyites, like Pinay and Laurens, had a few years out of politics after 1942 before resuming their careers.
53 Rémond, op. cit., pp. 308–9.
54 Griffiths, op. cit., p. 337.
55 For a general discussion, see Péllissier, op. cit., pp. 323–31.
56 Anderson, op. cit., p. 275; see Ousby, op. cit., pp. 313–14.
57 Williams, op. cit., pp. 17–19 and pp. 386–95. See also Shennan (1989), op. cit., Chapter 4, 'De Gaulle and the parties at the Liberation', for sections on the main three parties; see also B. D. Graham, *The French Socialists and Tripartisme 1944–1947* (Weidenfeld and Nicolson, London, 1965), especially Chapter 3.
58 Rousso (1994), op. cit., p. 16.
59 T. Judt, *Past Imperfect: French Intellectuals 1944–1956* (University of California Press, Oxford, 1992), p. 45.
60 Rousso (1994), op. cit., pp. 16–18.

61 Rousso (1994), op. cit., p. 18, plus my ideas (I have built upon Rousso's initial ideas).
62 A point developed from Rousso (1994), op. cit., p. 18.
63 Judt, op. cit., pp. 46–7.
64 McMillan, op. cit., p. 149.
65 Larkin, op. cit., p. 119.
66 McMillan, op. cit., p. 149.
67 Rousso (1994), op. cit., Chapter 3.
68 Webster, op. cit., p. 68.
69 *Independent*, 24 March 1990.
70 Lottman (1986), op. cit., p. 285.
71 *Daily Telegraph*, 25 November 1990.
72 *Independent on Sunday*, 24 March 1991.
73 Headlines in the British press.
74 *Independent on Sunday*, 24 March 1991.
75 *Daily Telegraph*, 25 November 1990. For Bousquet in general see also J. Laughland, *The Death of Politics: France under Mitterrand* (Michael Joseph, London, 1994), pp. 218–20.
76 *Independent*, 25 May 1987.
77 *Independent*, 25 May 1989.
78 *Independent*, 24 March 1990.
79 *Sunday Times*, 28 May 1989.
80 *Independent*, 24 March 1990.
81 *Independent*, 31 May 1989.
82 See Gildea, op. cit., pp. 72–3.
83 Webster, op. cit., p. 214.
84 On the book see E. Duhamel, 'François Mitterrand between Vichy and the Resistance' in M. Maclean (ed.), *The Mitterrand Years* (Macmillan, London, 1998), p. 229. The controversial book by Pierre Péan was called *Une jeunesse française: François Mitterrand 1934–1947*.
85 See Duhamel, op. cit., p. 217; see also J. W. Friend, *The Long Presidency* (Westview, Oxford, 1998), pp. 9–10.
86 Friend, op. cit., p. 9.
87 *The Times*, 9 January 1996.
88 *Daily Telegraph*, 9 January 1996.
89 *Independent*, 9 January 1996.
90 R. Cole, *François Mitterrand* (Routledge, London, 1994); see also Laughland, op. cit., pp. 205–22.
91 See D. MacShane, *François Mitterrand*, Chapter 3 (Quartet, London, 1982), pp. 25–37.
92 Burrin, op. cit., p. 467.

93 Fenby, op. cit., p. 53.
94 Webster, op. cit., p. 217.
95 Webster, op. cit., pp. 214–16.
96 See Wright (1964), op. cit.
97 Kedward and Wood, op. cit., p. ix.

Evaluation: issues and themes

1 Sweets, op. cit.
2 Gough and Horne, op. cit., pp. 9–17.

Bibliography

J. Adler, *The Jews of Paris and the Final Solution* (OUP, Oxford, 1989).

M. Agulhon, *The French Republic 1879–1992* (Blackwell, Oxford, 1995).

L. Allen, 'Resistance and the Catholic Church in France', in S. Hawes and R. White, *Resistance in Europe: 1939–45* (Penguin, London, 1976).

H. Amouroux, *Le 18 Juin 40* (Fayard, Paris, 1990).

M. Anderson, *Conservative Politics in France* (Allen and Unwin, London, 1974).

C. Andrieu, 'Les résistantes, perspectives de recherche' in A. Prost (ed.), *La Résistance, une histoire sociale* (Les Editions de l'Atelier, Paris, 1997).

J. Ardagh, *France in the New Century* (Viking, London, 1999).

'Art and culture under the Occupation' (*Hidden Hands* documentary, Channel 4, 1996).

N. Atkin, *Pétain* (Longman, London, 1998).

N. Atkin and F. Tallett, *Religion, Society and Politics in France since 1789* (Hambledon, London, 1991).

J.-P. Azéma and F. Bédarida (eds), *La France des années noires* (Seuil, Paris, 1993).

D. Bair, *Simone de Beauvoir: A Biography* (Vintage, London, 1991).

S. Barber, *Weapons of Liberation* (Faber and Faber, London, 1996).

M. O. Baruch, *Servir l'état français* (Fayard, Paris, 1997).

S. de Beauvoir, *The Prime of Life* (Penguin, London, 1960).

F. Bédarida, 'De Gaulle and the Resistance 1940–1944' in H. Gough and J. Horne (eds), *De Gaulle and Twentieth Century France* (Edward Arnold, London, 1994).

A. Beevor and A. Cooper, *Paris after the Liberation* (Hamish Hamilton, London, 1994).

A. Beltran, R. Frank and H. Rousso, *La Vie des enterprises sous l'occupation* (Belin, Paris, 1994).

F. Bertin, *Rennes sous l'occupation* (Ouest France, Rennes, c. 1981).

P. Birnbaum, *La France aux français* (Seuil, Paris, 1993).

F. Bloch-Lainé and C. Gruson, *Hauts fonctionnaires sous l'occupation* (Odile Jacob, Paris, 1996).

H. Le Boterf, *La Vie parisienne sous l'occupation* (France-Empire, Paris, 1997).

R. Bouderon and G. Willard, *1940: De la défaite à la résistance* (Messidor, Paris, 1990).

F. Braudel (Foreword) – *Les annéees trente de la crise a la guerre* (Seuil, Paris, 1983).

P. Burrin, *Living with Defeat* (Seuil, London, 1991).

A. Cady, 'Discourses of Resistance' in M. Scriven and P. Wagstaff (eds), *War and Society in Twentieth Century France* (Berg, Oxford, 1991).

G. Chauvy, *Histoire secrète de l'occupation* (Payot, Paris, 1991).

L. Cheles, R. Ferguson and M. Vaughan (eds), *Neo-Fascism in Europe* (Longman, London, 1991).

C. Chevrillon, *Une résistance ordinaire* (Félin, Paris, 1999).

A. Cobban, *A History of Modern France, Volume 3: 1871–1962* (Penguin, London, 1982).

R. Cole, *François Mitterrand* (Routledge, London, 1994).

R. Cole, *A Traveller's History of France* (Windrush, Moreton-in-Marsh, 1996).

M. Collins Weitz, *Sisters in the Resistance* (Wiley, Toronto, 1995).

B. Comte, *Une utopie combattante* (Fayard, Paris, 1991).

D. Cook, *Charles de Gaulle: A Biography* (Putnam, London, 1983).

A. Copley, *Sexual Moralities in France* (Routledge, London, 1992).

J. Corbett, *Through French Windows* (University of Michigan Press, Michigan, 1997).

J.-P. Le Crom, *Syndicats nous voilà! Vichy et le corporatisme* (Atelier, Paris, 1995).

B. Crozier, *De Gaulle: The Statesman* (Methuen, London, 1973).

Daily Telegraph newspaper.

J. Dalloz, *La France de la libération* (Presses Universitaires de France, Paris, 1983).

M. Déat, *Mémoires politiques* (Denoël, Paris, 1989).

A. Debon, *La Mission helmsman* (Harmattan, Paris, 1997).

J. Defrasne, *Histoire de la collaboration* (Presses Universitaires de France, 1982).

J. Defrasne, *L'Occupation allemande en France* (Presses Universitaires de France, Paris, 1985).

J. Delperrie de Bayac, *Histoire de la milice 2: Les assassins de l'ordre* (Fayard, Paris, 1969).

F. Delpla, *Montoire* (Albin Michel, Paris, 1996).

A. W. Deporte, *De Gaulle's Foreign Policy 1944–1946* (Harvard University Press, Cambridge, Mass., 1968).

H. Diamond, 'The everyday experience of women during the Second World War in the Toulouse region' in M. Scriven and P. Wagstaff (eds), *War and Society in Twentieth Century France* (Berg, Oxford, 1991).

L. Douzou, *La Désobedience: histoire du mouvement libération-sud* (Odile Jacob, Paris, 1995).

F.-G. Dreyfus, *Histoire de Vichy* (Perrin, Paris, 1990).

F.-G. Dreyfus, *Histoire de la resistance* (Fallois, Paris, 1996).

E. Duhamel, 'François Mitterrand between Vichy and the Resistance' in M. Maclean (ed.), *The Mitterrand Years* (Macmillan, London, 1998).

Études sur la France de 1939 à nos jours (Seuil, Paris, 1985).

J. Fenby, *On the Brink* (Little, Brown, London, 1998).

M. Ferro, *Pétain* (Fayard, Paris, 1987).

H. Footitt and J. Simmonds, 'The politics of liberation: France 1943–1945' in M. Scriven and P. Wagstaff, *War and Society in Twentieth Century France* (Berg, Oxford, 1991).

Franco-German Armistice, 22 June 1940, reprinted in D. Thomson (ed.), *Empire and Republic* (Harper and Row, London, 1968).

J. W. Friend, *The Long Presidency* (Westview, Oxford, 1998).

F. Garçon, *De Blum à Petain* (Cerf, Paris, 1984).

C. de Gaulle, *War Memoirs*, Volume 1 (Collins, London, 1959).

R. Gildea, *France since 1945* (OUP, Oxford, 1996).

P. Goubert, *The Course of French History* (Routledge, London, 1991).

H. Gough and J. Horne (eds), *De Gaulle and Twentieth Century France* (Edward Arnold, London, 1994).

B. D. Graham, *The French Socialists and Tripartisme 1944–1947* (Weidenfeld and Nicolson, London, 1965).

R. Griffin, *The Nature of Fascism* (Routledge, London, 1994).

R. Griffiths, *Pétain* (Constable, London, 1970).

P. Guidoni and R. Verdier (eds), *Les Socialistes en résistance* (Seli Arslan, Paris, 1999).

W. D. Halls, *Politics, Society and Christianity in Vichy France* (Berg, Oxford, 1995).

A. G. Hargreaves (ed.), *Immigration in Post-War France* (Methuen, London, 1987).

A. Hartley, *Gaullism* (Routledge and Kegan, London, 1972).

S. Hawes, 'The individual and the Resistance community in France' in S. Hawes and R. White, *Resistance in Europe 1939–45* (Penguin, London, 1976).

S. Hazareesingh, *Political Traditions in Modern France* (OUP, Oxford, 1996).

N. Hewlett, *Modern French Politics* (Polity, Cambridge, 1998).

I. Higgins, 'France, soil and language: some Resistance poems by Luc Berimont and Jean Marcenac' in R. Kedward and R. Austin, *Vichy France and Resistance* (Croom Helm, London, 1985).

G. Hirschfeld and P. Marsh, *Collaboration in France* (Berg, Oxford, 1989).

A. Horne, *The French Army and Politics: 1870–1970* (Macmillan, London, 1984).

J. A. Huston, *Across the Face of France* (University Press of America, London, 1984).

P. Hyman, *From Dreyfus to Vichy* (New York, Columbia University Press, 1979).

Independent newspaper.

Independent on Sunday newspaper.

J. Isorni, *Le Condamné de la citadelle* (Flammarion, Paris, 1982).

J. Jackson, *De Gaulle* (Cardinal, London, 1990).

P. Jankowski, *Communism and Collaboration: Simon Sabiani and Politics in Marseille 1919–44* (Yale University Press, New Haven and London, 1989).

L. Joxe, *Victoires sur la nuit* (Flammarion, Paris, 1981).

T. Judt, *Past Imperfect: French Intellectuals 1944–1956* (University of California Press, Oxford, 1992).

A. Kaspi, *La Libération de la France* (Perrin, Paris, 1995).

H. R. Kedward, 'Behind the polemics: French communists and Resistance 1939–41' in S. Hawes and R. White, *Resistance in Europe: 1939–45* (Penguin, London, 1976).

H. R. Kedward, *Resistance in Vichy France* (OUP, Oxford, 1978).

H. R. Kedward, 'The Maquis and the culture of the outlaw' in H. R. Kedward and R. Austin, *Vichy France and the Resistance* (Croom Helm, London, 1985).

H. R. Kedward, *Occupied France* (Blackwell, Oxford, 1989).

H. R. Kedward, 'The Maquis: whose history?' in M. Scriven and P. Wagstaff (eds), *War and Society in Twentieth Century France* (Berg, Oxford, 1991).

H. R. Kedward, *In Search of the Maquis: Rural Resistance in Southern France 1942–44* (Clarendon, Oxford, 1994).

H. R. Kedward and N. Wood (eds), *The Liberation of France* (Berg, Oxford, 1995).

P. J. Kingston, *Anti-semitism in France during the 1930s* (University of Hull, Hull, 1983).

F. Knight, *The French Resistance 1940–4* (Lawrence and Wishart, London, 1975).

A. Kriegel and S. Courtois, *Eugen Fried* (Seuil, Paris, 1997).

R. Kuisel, *Seducing the French* (University of California, Berkeley, 1996).

J. Lacouture, *De Gaulle: The Rebel 1890–1944* (Norton, London, 1990).

W. Laqueur (ed.), *Fascism: A Reader's Guide* (Penguin, London, 1982).

M. Larkin, *France since the Popular Front* (Clarendon, Oxford, 1991).

C. Laubier (ed.), *The Condition of Women in France: 1945 to the Present* (Routledge, London, 1990).

J. Laughland, *The Death of Politics: France under Mitterrand* (Michael Joseph, London, 1991).

A. Laurens, *Les Rivaux de Charles de Gaulle: La bataille de la légitimité en France de 1940 à 1944* (Robert Laffont, Paris, 1977).

P. Laval, *The Unpublished Diary of Pierre Laval* (Falcon, London, 1948).

B. Lecornu, *Un Préfet sous l'occupation allemande* (France-Empire, Paris, 1984).

S. J. Lee, *The European Dictatorships 1918–1945* (Routledge, London, 1994).

J.-P. Levy, *Memoires d'un franc-tireur* (Complexe, Paris, 1998).

L. Lévy, *France is a Democracy* (Victor Gollancz, London, 1942).

H. Lottman, *The People's Anger: Justice and Revenge in Post-Liberation France* (Hutchinson, London, 1986).

H. Lottman, *The Left Bank* (Halo, San Francisco, 1991).

J. S. McLelland (ed.), *The French Right* (Jonathan Cape, London, 1961).

J. F. McMillan, *Twentieth Century France* (Edward Arnold, London, 1992).

D. MacShane, *François Mitterrand*, Chapter 3 (Quartet, London, 1982).

M. Marrus and R. Paxton, *Vichy France and the Jews* (Stanford University Press, Stanford, 1995).

C. Mauriac, *The Other De Gaulle* (Angus and Robertson, London, 1973).

A. Maurois, *A History of France* (Jonathan Cape, London, 1960).

H. Michel and B. Markine-Guetzévitch, *Les Ideés politiques et sociales de la résistance* (Presses Universitaires de France, Paris, 1954).

H. Michel, B. Mirkine-Guetzévitch and D. Mayer (eds), *La France sous l'occupation* (Presses Universitaires de France, Paris, 1959).

H. Michel, *Histoire de la France libre* (Presses Universitaires de France, Paris, 1963).

H. Michel, *Histoire de la résistance en France* (Presses Universitaires de France, Paris, 1965).

H. Michel, *Paris allemand* (Albin Michel, Paris, 1981).

P. Milza, *Fascisme français* (Flammarion, Paris, 1987).

J. Monnet, *Memoirs* (Collins, London, 1978).

A. Morris, *Collaboration and Resistance Reviewed* (Berg, New York, 1992).

'Myths and memories of World War II', BBC2, 1996.

C. Nettelbeck (ed.), *War and Identity: The French and the Second World War* (Routledge, London, 1994).

J. Nobécourt, *Une histoire politique de l'armée (1) 1919–1942* (Seuil, Paris, 1967).

H. Noguères, M. Degliame-Fouché and J.-L. Vigier, *Histoire de la résistance en France de 1940 à 1945, Vol. 1 June 1940–June 1941* (Robert Laffont, Paris, 1967).

A. Nouschi and M. Agulhon, *La France de 1914 à 1940* (Nathan, Paris, c. 1984).

P. Ory (ed.), *La France allemande: paroles du collaborationnisme français* (1933–1945) (Gallimard/Julliard, Paris, 1977).

P. Ory, *Les Collaborateurs 1940–1945* (Seuil, Paris, 1976).

S. M. Osgood (ed.), *The Fall of France, 1940* (Heath, London, 1965).

I. Ousby, *Occupation: The Ordeal of France 1940–1944* (John Murray, London, 1998).

P. Ouston, *France in the Twentieth Century* (Macmillan, London, 1972).

M. Parrotin, *Le Temps du Maquis* (2nd edition, 1981).

R. Paxton, *Vichy France: Old Guard and New Order 1940–1944* (Columbia University Press, New York, 1982).

A. Pedley, *As Mighty as the Sword: A Study of the Writings of Charles de Gaulle* (Elm Bank, Exeter, 1996).

P. Péllissier, *Philippe Pétain* (Hachette, Paris, 1980).

R. Price, *A Concise History of France* (CUP, Cambridge, 1993).

A. Prost (ed.), *La Résistance, une histoire sociale* (Les Editions de l'Atelier, Paris, 1997).

R. Rémond, *The Right Wing in France* (University of Pennsylvania Press, Philadelphia, 1971).

Rémy, *Le 10 Mai 1940: Chronique d'une guerre perdue 2* (Editions France-Empire, Paris, 1980).

J.-P. Rioux, *The Fourth Republic 1944–1958* (CUP, Cambridge, 1989).

D. Rossignol, *Vichy et les francs-maçons* (Lattès, Paris, 1981).

G. Rossi-Landi, *La Drôle de guerre* (Armand Colin, Paris, 1971).

H. Rousso, *Les années noires: vivre sous l'occupation* (Gallimard, Paris, 1992).

H. Rousso, *The Vichy Syndrome* (Harvard University Press, Cambridge, Mass., 1994).

J.-P. Sartre, *Paris sous l'occupation* (Gallimard, Paris, 1949).

D. Schoenbrun, *Maquis* (Robert Hale, London, 1990).

M. Scriven and P. Wagstaff (eds), *War and Society in Twentieth Century France* (Berg, Oxford, 1991).

A. Shennan, *Rethinking France* (OUP, Oxford, 1989).

A. Shennan, *De Gaulle* (Longman, London, 1993).

W. L. Shirer, *The Collapse of the Third Republic* (Da Capo Press, New York, 1994).

Y. R. Simon, *The Road to Vichy 1918–1938* (University Press of America, London, 1988).

J.-F. Sirinelli (ed.), *Les Droites françaises* (Gallimard, Paris, 1992).

Sunday Times newspaper.

J. F. Sweets, *Choices in Vichy France* (OUP, New York, 1994).

R. Thalmann, *La Mise au pas* (Fayard, Paris, 1991).

D. Thomson (ed.), *Empire and Republic* (Harper and Row, London, 1968).

The Times newspaper.

H. Tint, *France since 1918* (Batsford, London, 1970).

T. Todorov and A. Jacquet, *Guerre et paix sous l'occupation* (Arléa, Paris, 1996).

E. Tolansky, 'Les cahiers du silence' in R. Kedward and R. Austin, *Vichy France and the Resistance* (Croom Helm, London, 1985).

D. Veillon, *Le Franc-Tireur* (Flammarion, Paris, 1977).

Vercors, *The Silence of the Sea*, J. Brown and L. Stokes (eds), (Berg, Oxford, 1993).

P. Webster, *Pétain's Crime* (Papermac, London, 1994).

A. Werth, *France 1940–1955* (Robert Hale, London, 1957).

A. Werth, *De Gaulle* (Penguin, London, 1969).

O. Wieviorka, *Une certaine idée de la résistance* (Seuil, Paris, 1995).

P. Williams, *Politics in Post-War France* (Longmans, London, 1958).

M. Winock, *Nationalisme, antisémitisme et fascisme en France* (Seuil, Paris, 1990).

M. Winock, *Histoire de l'Éxtrême droite en France* (Seuil, Paris, 1994).

R. S. Wistrich, *Anti-Semitism* (Mandarin, London, 1992).

G. Wright, *Rural Revolution in France* (OUP, London, 1964).

G. Wright, *France in Modern Times* (Norton, London, 1995).

S. Zuccotti, *The Holocaust, the French, and the Jews* (Basic Books, New York, 1999).

Index